Toward a Biblical Theology of Marriage

Toward a Biblical Theology of Marriage

A Study of the Bible's Vocabulary of Marriage

ERNEST D. MARTIN

WIPF & STOCK · Eugene, Oregon

TOWARD A BIBLICAL THEOLOGY OF MARRIAGE
A Study of the Bible's Vocabulary of Marriage

Wipf & Stock
An Imprint of Wipf and Stock Publishers
199 W. 8th Ave., Suite 3
Eugene, OR 97401

www.wipfandstock.com

ISBN 13: 978-1-60899-332-1

Manufactured in the U.S.A.

Dedicated to those with the challenge and opportunity
to uphold the biblical paradigm of marriage.

Contents

Foreword

IT IS NO SECRET that the "institution" of marriage is in turmoil, and the church is not exempt from the trauma. As a pastor, I have had many books recommended with the claim to have answers for the crisis we are in. Some of these books have been helpful, but very few are written with pastors in mind. This work, *Toward a Biblical Theology of Marriage*, provides a biblical study for pastors that essentially lets the Bible speak for itself. Ernest Martin's approach is not an attempt to win an argument. Instead he is driven by the question, "But what does the Bible really say?" As one who accepts that God has spoken and continues to speak to us through the Scriptures, it is refreshing to have in hand a study that allows the Bible to speak to this specific issue. I am in full agreement with his "belief that the Bible does intersect with life in any age."

Ernest's approach is to embrace the total package of what Scripture has to say regarding marriage, not avoiding difficult or complex passages. He has walked into this library of information on what the Bible says regarding marriage and has organized it in a way that helps us make sense of what we read. An example of this is the chapter titled "Intra-canonical Continuity and Movement." He provides insight into the struggle of maintaining God's intention for marriage from the beginning (Genesis) while living in the context of surrounding cultures and practices. How often have Christians and pastors been challenged with questions as to why polygamy seemed to be acceptable in the Old Testament and yet is clearly discouraged in the New Testament? While not limited to the issue of biblical marriage, the struggle of maintaining God's intention while living in the context of surrounding cultures and practices remains a current challenge.

This is not a "quick fix" book; it is about long-range and long-term correction in the way we think and teach. Most would agree that current trends and behaviors are not working, but few understand how far off track we in the church have strayed from biblical intention. This study has the potential of improving and affecting marriages for generations to come, but only if we move toward a more biblical theology in how we think and in how we teach. I am hopeful that our children, and our children's children, will see firsthand a more biblical model for marriage than what many currently experience.

Perhaps the greatest strength this book has to offer is that it has not been dumbed down for the sake of sales to everyone, nor has it been written at such an exclusive level that very few can comprehend it. It is written to pastors—pastors who are tired of seeing marriages fail and who are certain God's word provides answers. It is a useful tool, and anyone who has ever worked in a blue-collar occupation knows the benefit of a high-quality tool that can be put to use on a daily basis. If we begin to speak and teach and live out in our own marriages what God intended from the beginning, we will once again be taken seriously. It is with joy and hope for the marriages that will one day be that I commend this work for the ministry to which God has called you.

James E. Bartholomew
Pastor, Dayspring Christian Fellowship
Massillon, Ohio

Preface

Bᴏᴏᴋs ᴀʙᴏᴜᴛ ᴍᴀʀʀɪᴀɢᴇ ᴀʙᴏᴜɴᴅ, but few of them are giving seri-ous consideration to a theology of marriage. While on the one hand some books about marriage assume that the Bible has definitive directives on the issues of marriage, other contemporary writings reflect the notion that the Bible is not really relevant to the issues of marriage in this millennium.

My motivations for exploring a theology of marriage based on biblical revelation stem from a belief that the Bible does intersect with life in any age. That is not to say that selected texts of the Bible can be pasted into the current scene without regard for the context or the unfolding flow of revelation. The fruit of my study is intentionally entitled *Toward a Biblical Theology of Marriage*. It does not fit a strict definition of biblical theology as distinct from systematic or historical theology. It does pay attention to movement within the canon, specifically Genesis 1 and 2, the rest of the Old Testament, and the New Testament. It traces experience, teachings, and developments from beginnings to the marriage of the Lamb. The initial and primary focus has been on the biblical vocabulary associated with marriage. I have not found that this approach has been at the heart of previous studies, at least not published studies. Exegesis of key texts became necessary. These are the data out of which a biblical theology is discerned. The observations, sometimes thematic, rise out of the biblical data itself. It is not an exercise in looking for details that fit an imposed outline.

This pursuit has been primarily self-motivated, with encouragement from several biblical scholars. I have worked on this project, off and on, for more than ten years. I tried to be as objective as possible, open to what I might find, rather than looking for support for what I thought the Scriptures would say or what I wanted them to say. Goshen (IN) College professors introduced me to inductive Bible study many decades ago. I adapted an inductive approach to the biblical vocabulary entailed in this study. I have maintained over the years the Hebrew and Greek language skills acquired in Goshen College Biblical Seminary classes and enhanced them. My personal library had many of the resources needed for this study. Seminary libraries had more needed resources. More sources have been consulted than are listed in the bibliography.

Bible study should normally turn up some things unanticipated, and that has been the case in this study. Several unifying themes and "aha's" have emerged far beyond expectations. The findings have been shared and tested with several Pastor Peer Groups. Feedback from several readers has led to some major reorganization of the material to increase readability.

Then, having about given up trying to get this study published, a mutual acquaintance connected me with a pastor in Switzerland who is addressing issues of marriage in his context. His insights and interest in my work reignited my interest in pursuing a publishable manuscript. Coming across additional facets of the subject has led to revisions and expansions over the many years I have worked on this study.

Who, then, may benefit from this volume? The broad strokes are available to any serious reader. Since a major part of the study had to do with biblical vocabulary associated with marriage, in both Hebrew and Greek, some details call for acquaintance with these ancient languages. The more technical aspects of the vocabulary review will be found in an appendix. Some grammatical details are noted within the main text. These details needed to be included to show how findings have been arrived at, rather than simply stating conclusions. The primary target readership is pastors and counselors with at least some skills in biblical languages. But since Hebrew and Greek words are transliterated, many persons interested in the subject will be able to follow the exploration, findings, and implications of the study. Seminary students and professors have also been in mind in the writing.

As indicated in the outline, the first section surveys the current marriage scene, highlighting why a theology of marriage arising out of biblical revelation is crucial for the church now. A block is devoted to the nature of this aspect of biblical theology and the challenges of such a quest. The main part of the book lists and explains findings and affirmations arising out of the study. Comparison of the unfolding biblical scene with the cultures surrounding the Old Testament and New Testament serves to enable the reader to note the similarities and significant differences. A final section addresses how the church can relate these theological understandings to persons in the several categories of relationship to marriage.

Many persons have lent their encouragement, insightful observations, and questions. These include several pastors' groups, Gerald W. Kaufman, Jacob W. Elias, Willard M. Swartley, Cheryl Vanatsky, Philip K. Clemens, Larry D. Rohrer, Perry B. Yoder, Christoph Monsch-Rinderknecht, Samuel Olarawaju, and James E. Bartholomew, who agreed to write a foreword. Several persons have made significant monetary contributions toward bringing this project to publication.

This study does not have a definitive end. At many places the comments could be expanded. Although I keep coming across things I want to add or modify, there comes a time to stop writing and send it on. I have a growing sense that what has emerged in my study can contribute to the strengthening of marriage in this time, and to the conversations about how biblical revelation is understood and brought to intersect with the current questions about what God intends. The focus is not on putting down alternative views, but on occasion I note where/how these observations have bearing on marriage issues, past and present. I am making the case for marriage as I have come to understand biblical revelation and doing so in positive terms. My desire is to honor Christ and his body.

Ernest D. Martin
2009

Abbreviations

TECHNICAL

adj.	adjective
cf.	compare
e.g.	for example
et al.	and others
f.	feminine
fut.	future
ibid.	in the same place
imperf.	imperfect
impv.	imperative
indic.	Indicative
infin.	Infinitive
lit.	literally
m.	masculine
mid.	middle
neut.	neuter gender
n. d.	no date
n.	noun
p(p).	page(s)
par(s).	paragraph(s)
pf.	perfect tense
pl.	plural
subj.	subjunctive
v./vv.	verse/verses
vb.	verb

TRANSLATIONS

EDM	Author's translation
KJV	King James Version
NAB	New American Bible
NASB	New American Standard Bible
NIV	New International Version
NRSV	New Revised Standard Version
RSV	Revised Standard Version
TNIV	Today's New International Version

1

Who Needs One?

ALMOST ALL CULTURES HAVE and perpetuate the practice of marriage as a formal basis for cohabiting. Ceremonies and mores vary, but the cultural assumption goes on that marriage is a given for human life. Historically marriage was primarily a family event. Roman Catholicism (followed by some other traditions) has made marriage a sacrament, thus giving it a strong ecclesiastical bent. Calvinism has focused on marriage as covenant. Lutheranism has viewed marriage as an order of creation to restrain sexual sin but with no role in salvation. Probably more by default than intention, much of Protestantism and society in general leave the definitions and the regulation of marriage primarily as a function of the state. At this writing, the United States Internal Revenue Service, operating under federal law (Defense of Marriage Act, 1996), says who is married and who is single for taxation purposes. Even though several states now legalize same-gender marriages, those couples must file as single persons with the IRS, with resultant higher taxes than if filing as married. Although ministers and churches may (and should) require premarital counseling, all other requirements are specified by the state in which the marriage takes place. Officiating ministers need to be registered with the state to make the marriage legal. We have allowed ourselves to be confined to legal definitions of marriage, without at least equal time for a theological perspective.

Common law marriage, recognized in some states, rests on a slightly different definition of marriage. Cohabitation in itself does not constitute marriage. Where the status known as common law marriage is recognized, it cannot be dissolved with "common law divorce" apart from due legal proceedings.

Although marriage continues to be held as society's ideal, it is increasingly the case that couples live together without the benefit of formal or legal marriage. What was once commonly regarded as "holy matrimony" has come to be considered by many as "a take-it-or-leave-it piece of paper." The 2000 census reports 5.5 million unmarried partner homes, about 5 percent of all homes, which is up from 3 percent in 1990. The number of women raising children without fathers around was up by 25 percent in the decade.[1] Babies born "out of wedlock" seem to raise fewer and fewer eyebrows. One can hardly avoid the evidence that marriage, and consequently also family, is in deep trouble.

David Popenoe, in the State of Our Unions 2007 essay, "The Future of Marriage in America," says, "There can be no doubt that the institution of marriage has continued to weaken in recent years. . . . Fewer adult are married, more are divorced or remaining single, and more are living together outside of marriage or living alone. . . . Today, more children are born out-of-wedlock (now almost four out of ten), and more are living in stepfamilies, with cohabiting but unmarried adults, or with a single parent."[2] The increase of cohabitation without marriage accounts in a large part for the decline in the divorce rate in recent years. One anomaly in this scene has to do with age and length of marriage. "In 2006 the divorce rate among Americans over fifty was triple what it had been in the early 1990s. Longevity of marriage was no longer a factor in staying together, nor was age."[3]

Popenoe notes that the weakening of marriage is less pronounced in America than in European countries (especially northwestern Europe). The demise of Christendom is more advanced there than in America, as yet. The fading of institutional church power and influence, along with acceptance of secular individualism, correlates with the growing abandonment of marriage as a traditional institution.[4] The evidence is abundant that marriage, and consequently also family, is in deep trouble.

As one example, Christoph Monsch-Rinderknecht, a Swiss Reformed pastor, finds in his research that marriage in his country has moved from the traditionally accepted norm to marriage as convenience and now as love-marriage. In Switzerland, where the state has the exclusive right to marry, some couples choose to add a church ceremony to their civil mar-

---

1. Associated Press, "Census Records," 5A.

2. Popenoe, "Future of Marriage," 1.

3. Houghton, "Divorce and Age," 1.

4. Popenoe, "Future of Marriage," 1.

riage. Couples who do not have an active relationship with the church leave it as a civil matter or live together without any marriage formalities. His research in 2005 (part of his DMin project) projected that 52.6 percent of marriages in Switzerland will end in divorce. The fallout has devastating effects on children and on the future of marriage. With the church being increasingly sidelined, this pastor was led to provide pastoral colleagues with materials to use for marriage enrichment settings and for counseling those open to a church ceremony.[5] From a Christian perspective, finding a place to stand in this social confusion is imperative.

An increase in cohabitation without formal or legal marriage indicates a changing attitude toward marriage. Further evidence about the perceived value of marriage is found in the shortage of U.S.-born babies available for adoption. While there is a lamentable increase in abortion being used as a remedy for unplanned pregnancies, only 1 percent of women with unplanned pregnancies choose adoption. Many teen girls choose motherhood as single parents but for the wrong reasons. Their misguided choices are then reinforced by peers (schoolmates begging for copies of sonograms) and state agencies wanting to be of help but inadvertently making teen motherhood attractive. Babies/children being raised by grandmothers, although in some respects commendable, also adds to the deterioration of marriage and family values.

Fatherhood is also in trouble. An increasing absence of fathers in parenting children is disturbingly evident. Identified as the "male problematic" by Don Browning and others,[6] biological fathers are too often abandoning responsibilities toward their children and the mothers of their children. In broad terms this means many of today's children grow up without benefit of a male figure in their lives. The effects are disastrous for children. Research says children generally do better in about all ways if in a two-parent, intact family. One-gender parental arrangements beg the question: how do children in those "families" gain sexual identity and develop healthy cross-gender relationships?

Multiple factors contribute to this growing reality. Fathers do not automatically invest themselves in their sired children the way mothers do, who carry, bear, and care for their helpless offspring. In many cases the work culture in which fathers are involved distances them from their

5. Monsch-Rinderknecht, *Four Marriage.*

6. Browning, *Culture Wars.*

family (children and wife), in time, geography, and energy. A widely held assumption that it is the father's job to provide for the family and the mother's job to raise children justifies the father's absence in the parenting responsibilities. Sometimes a "female problematic" may be involved. The mother may, for a variety of supposed reasons, think she can be the best parent without a man involved. Her "man/men" (her father or the father[s] of her child/children) may have created that feeling. In the economic downturn of 2008–2009, more men than women have lost their jobs. As a result, gender roles have changed. Many more husbands/fathers are caring for their children, while the wives/mothers are gainfully employed. And the fathers are enjoying it!

While just about everybody agrees we have a serious problem, solutions are far from uniform. Opinions differ on what needs to be done to remedy the problem. A biblical theology of marriage that includes relationships between father and mother and the shape of a healthy parenting process is imperative if the church is to respond helpfully.

The social sciences have been calling attention to what is perceived to be a crisis for family. Many in these fields are now saying that the focus needs to be on marriage as the way to address the future for families. That, they say, will require the combined efforts of religion (with Christian faith having much to offer), social sciences and agencies, and the political arena.

The social sciences contribute valuable data and assessment of what is happening in marriage and family. Social sciences have also introduced the concept of "role" into husband/wife relationship. That translates into terms such as "a man's place" and "a woman's place" in the primary social unit of husband and wife. Neither the term nor the concept of "role" is to be found and delineated in the Bible. The concept is more skewing than helpful in coming to terms with the biblical texts in their settings. Robert M. Hicks writes, "Marriage roles determined by gender" is one of the common myths about family that is doing serious disservice. Although the concept is accepted uncritically, even by evangelical authors and speakers, Hicks contends that it has no basis in Scripture, and results in confusion and hurt.[7]

7. Hicks, *Christian Family,* 53–57. For further analysis of the status of marriage in the United States and abroad see: The National Marriage Project, www.marriage.rutgers .edu/; PBS documentary: "Marriage—Just a Piece of Paper?" www.marriagetv.uchicago .edu/; Marriage Movement, www.marriagemovement.org/; Council on Contemporary

Marriage has fallen into disrepute for a variety of reasons. One is the prevalence of domestic violence that has led to marriage being called a "hitting license." Violence within marriage and family won't stop by reaffirming a clearer definition of marriage, of course. But the reality of spouse abuse calls for comprehensive teaching on the marriage relationship as the primary social unit.

Among those examining what is happening to marriage and family as a result of modernization (industrialization and globalization) is Don S. Browning, Alexander Campbell professor emeritus of ethics and the social sciences at the University of Chicago Divinity School and director of the Lily Project on Religion, Culture, and Family. Browning sees a threat to marriage in modernization, "the spread throughout the world of technical rationality and its efficiency-oriented and cost-benefit logics and patterns," and globalization, "the process by which information, images, symbols, and styles of life zigzag back and forth across the world." He contends that these and related factors are having a disruptive effect on families everywhere. He is not calling for a turning back of the clock but a reconstruction of marriage and family, with religions, particularly Christianity, taking initiative in getting marriage on the agenda again. Browning envisions religious entities taking a proactive approach—not merely decrying the deterioration of marriage and family but promoting intentionality and solid meaning into marriage. Christianity uniquely contributes, he says, the trilogy of grace, forgiveness, and self-sacrifice.[8]

Another facet of the current scenario is the increased call for formalized recognition (and blessing) of same-gender extended contracts. One reason for exploring a theology of marriage is this hot issue of same-gender commitments. Although "marriage" has not yet been the fully accepted general terminology for such arrangements, the societal and legal direction is becoming increasingly clear. Several states now recognize these as on a par with marriage and are issuing marriage licenses to same-gender couples. Several denominations provide formal rituals for same-gender commitments. This shift has more to do with a redefinition of marriage than with including same-gender partnering under the umbrella of marriage. However, if the essentials (the defining ingredients) of marriage are that it be monogamous and lasting, as it is sometimes put,

---

Families, www.contemporaryfamilies.org/; INTAMS, International Academy for Marital Spirituality, www.intams.org/; and much more available on the Internet.

8. Browning, *Culture Wars*, 73–98; Browning, "Putting Marriage," 4.

these in themselves do not rule out same-gender contracts. Adding sex to the equation still leaves the door open.

You have likely already noticed that I have chosen not to confuse "sex" and "gender." Except in quotations, gender has to do with the male-female distinction, and sex means sexual activity.

David Coolidge, a research fellow at the Institute on Religion and Public Life, makes a poignant comment: "The self-proclaimed gay and lesbian lobby has made it clear that the definition of marriage is the core of the issue—they do not want to broaden marriage, they want to redefine it. The debate about same-sex marriage, therefore, is a debate about marriage. It also should be clear that the liberal and postmodern models of marriage are not creations of the gay and lesbian community. As more Americans have diluted or shifted their beliefs and moral values, the cultural definition of marriage has become unstable. This, more than anything, has opened the door to arguments for same-sex marriage."[9] In his analysis of shifting values, Coolidge does not even mention biblical understandings. But we cannot avoid asking, what is the shape of a biblical theology of marriage, and does the biblical understanding of marriage provide any different or additional defining factors?

Rather than trying to identify the minimum essentials for a relationship to be called marriage, should not the church be looking to biblical revelation for what Christian marriage is called to be? Legal marriage will likely continue to be defined by the state. The church is in need of upholding a biblical vision of the potential for marriage in God's big design. The difference is like the difference between asking what the minimum requirements are for going to heaven and what Jesus is providing and offering as abundant life, beginning now. Definitions tend to be minimalist. What we need is a vision of God's intent and provision with respect to marriage, from beginning to end.

A library search reveals that relatively little is being done in the field of a biblical theology of marriage. Books and articles are plentiful on how to have a good marriage (at least a better one) and how to have good sex in marriage. But little attention seems to be given to a biblical theology. Many authors and speakers mention Bible principles for marriage, but they do not address seriously the crying need for a message from the church grounded in biblical revelation. They rather champion principles

9. Coolidge, "Dilemma," pars. 18–19.

based on common sense and psychology, without showing how they find their basis in Scripture.

The same tendency prevails when the focus is broadened to family matters. For example, Robert M. Hicks notes that Dr. James Dobson concludes his book, *Dare to Discipline*, with: "From Genesis to Revelation there is a consistent foundation on which to build an effective philosophy of parent-child relationships."[10] Hicks comments that although he has no difficulty with that statement, the biblical foundation was not given in the book. Hicks assesses Focus on the Family, along with many other efforts to address family issues, as psychologizing family life with the assumption that common-sense principles are biblical without showing that in fact they stem from the Scriptures as a whole. Hicks also has concern about the increasing political orientation of Focus on the Family, shifting concern about traditional family values to the political arena rather than keeping the focus on spiritual and biblical values.[11]

A relativistic culture has little interest in norms, much less in absolutes. To the extent that the Bible is regarded as a book of outdated rules, there may not be much market for books on a theology of marriage. The deconstructionist bent of postmodernism, brushing aside traditional values without offering positive constructs, has led to society's "loss of coordinates." This mathematical analogy aptly describes the current confusion in which truth/right is what truth/right is for "me." At best rules for morality are written in the sands of the seashore.

As Vinoth Ramachandra, a Sri Lankan scholar, has put it, "Here it seems that postmodernism is simply modernism come home to roost. A movement that sought to guard the objectivity of truth from theological 'interference' has ended up doubting the very concept of truth. A movement that gloried in reason and exalted it above divine revelation has come to spurn the rational in every area of life. A movement that began with the divinization of the self has culminated in the loss of that very self."[12] A sense of purpose and direction is desperately needed for all of life, certainly including the area of marriage. In his analysis of pluralism and relativism, Ramachandra gets into the relationship between experience and doctrine. Noting that for some, love takes priority over

10. Dobson, *Dare to Discipline*, 250.

11. Hicks, *Christian Family*, 46–49.

12. Ramachandra, *Gods That Fail*, 12.

truth, he says, "To wrench love out of the context of truth is to turn it into something else."[13] That commentary is pertinent to the current issues of biblical revelation and marriage.

IT IS TIME TO SPEAK UP, IF WE KNOW WHAT TO SAY

Is not this the time for the Christian church to reaffirm and promote what we can discern about the Creator-Redeemer's intent and provision for marriage? At this time of foundering and searching regarding marital values, the opportunity is ripe, if not overripe, for holding forth the divine paradigm for marriage as revealed in Holy Writ. An ecumenical statement released in 2000, "A Christian Declaration on Marriage," voices concern about the state of marriage and encourages churches to strengthen marriage. For any proactive effort by the Christian church to make a difference, it will need to be undergirded with contemporary discernment and vigorous teaching of a biblical theology of marriage.

Another perspective surfaces in an article by Serene Jones, "Bounded Openness." The article is not at all focused on marriage but is a response to postmodernism and the church from a feminist perspective. When questioned by the author about the theme of the article, Kate, a generation-Xer, expressed her frustration of being left to decide on her own about life. She sensed that as a Christian there ought to be more, but she didn't know where. Then after working with Habitat for Humanity, rebuilding a house with the know-how of an old carpenter, she added:

> I feel like our generation is standing in the rubble of demolished houses hoping someone shows up to help us figure out how to build something beautiful and safe. We don't have much theological know-how; we aren't immersed in a faith tradition that needs to be undone because we have not been religiously traditioned. We need someone to share with us the wisdom, the know-how, the basic rules of community—because we don't know those anymore. It seems to me that the basic stories, practices, and belief of the Christian faith can be that for our generation. The trick is that the church needs to show up on the site of the previous, demolished house and not spend all its time bemoaning the demolition, but instead put its energy into helping us creatively build a new house (knowing all along that many of the rules that built the previous house will still apply). In other words, that old carpenter represent-

13. Ramachandra, *Recovery*, 21.

ed, for me, the structures that postmodernism lacks and feminism seeks, structures the church can provide.[14]

Some aspects of this paragraph may not seem to fit the marriage issue. Some of the assumptions and myths about marriage do need to be exposed and challenged. The construction figure is certainly apropos of envisioning how the church can respond to the voids and rubble in marital understandings and practices.

These are not times to bemoan the erosion of marriage, or to engage in false nostalgia about "how it used to be." They are times begging for creative initiatives in response to the challenges emerging out of some segments of our society. A generation that has seen too much divorce may well be open to learning what it takes for marriage to work. The church can and must take advantage of opportunities to help. But we had better be doing our homework in biblical revelation and understandings. Reruns won't cut it.

14. Jones, "Bounded Openness," 49–55.

2

The Quest

A. QUESTIONS CALLING FOR ANSWERS

The goal of this research has been to discern in the Scriptures a biblical understanding of marriage. Bible study is fraught with the subjectivity of finding what one wants to find. I have tried to state the following questions as open-ended as possible, not implying desired conclusions. The guiding questions include these:

1. What defining factors come together to indicate what the essence is of the marriage relationship as revealed in Scripture?

2. What evidence is there of a divine intent for marriage?

3. Is there evidence of movement in an understanding of marriage within the canon, and if there is, are there distinguishing features of the contribution of Christ and the New Testament?

4. For whom is marriage a choice recognized by God?

5. What are the provisions for fulfilling marriage that stand alongside any perceived divine intent?

6. What is God's view of singleness, and are there specifications?

7. What, if anything, can damage, destroy, or terminate a marriage relationship, and why?

8. What does the church have to offer that is based on a thoroughly biblical understanding of marriage? What fundamentals translate beyond the world/culture of the Bible?

9. What paradigms does the Bible offer that can inform what Christian marriage—marriage between Christians and blessed by the church—is meant to be?

10. What is the biblical understanding of the relationship of marriage and parenting?

11. What help, if any, is there for the church facing the challenge of championing a heightened view of marriage and at the same time extending a redemptive ministry to those whose marriages have failed?

12. What is there about the biblical understanding of marriage that has a potential for speaking to those of the "postmodern" culture who seem to know intuitively that there must be somewhere a positive construct for marriage and family?

B. THE NATURE OF THE BIBLICAL DATA

Discerning a biblical understanding of marriage has its built-in challenges. The biblical material bristles with perplexities that caution the theologian to proceed carefully and humbly. If we turn to the Bible to find portraits of the ideal marriage and family, we are in for a surprise. The true-to-life accounts are far from ideal. For example, who would take as models Adam and Eve (after their sin), Noah, Abraham, Jacob, David, Solomon, or Hosea? In the Bible there is no specific command to get married and no comprehensive treatment of the meaning and intent of marriage. The people of God did not produce a marriage manual anywhere along the way. A biblical theology of marriage must take shape out of several sources.

First, we must look at vocabulary employed to speak of marriage and all that is related to it in the Hebrew Old Testament, the Septuagint (LXX), and the Greek New Testament. This has been the central focus of this study. Incidentally, the term "marriage" in the Bible almost always refers to the wedding, and not as in contemporary English, to the on-going relationship or state of matrimony. However, the terms "married" and "unmarried" are generally used as we use them. Shades of meaning underlie word choices, and these nuances shed light on understandings of marriage. (More below in the section on methods employed.)

Second, we must look at narrative material (what is reported as practiced). The story form is characteristic of Hebrew thought and writing. The Hebrews were not given to philosophical abstractions. Ask Hebrews about their beliefs, and they are likely to tell you stories. (Jesus's use of parables follows the pattern.) The language itself, based as it is on verbs rather than nouns, focuses on action rather than on ideas. With the expanse of history included in the biblical story, it is not surprising that shifts are evident in the phenomenological data, particularly in the Old Testament, and practices do not all accord with specific commands. (Examples to be explored later include movement into and later away from polygamy, sacred prostitution, and depreciative views of women.) It is not always entirely clear whether the wording related in the narrative is to be understood as descriptive (what is or will be) or prescriptive (what is supposed to be).

The historical setting for any given text (both narrative and specific rules and regulations) should be taken into account. The issues at the time of writing, editing, and compiling—not easily discerned—were likely different from those implied in the accounts themselves. These factors are part of the "ground-route" of hermeneutics, as over against the "air-route" of applying a contextualized part of the written word to times centuries and millennia later. We should not ignore the fact that neither Jesus nor Paul was married or had children. We need to take care in pasting their teachings into our contemporary milieu. But that does not mean judging the biblical material to be hopelessly outdated.

Discerning what needs to go into a biblical theology hinges on a defining view of Scripture. Joel B. Green identifies a critical perspective with respect to much of the Bible being in narrative form: "Despite widespread efforts either to distill theological claims from narrative or to deny that theology can be derived from narrative, we must recognize that narrative in scripture is a mode of theological discourse. . . . Rather than restricting scripture's role in theology to that of 'foundation' or 'source,' it is important to recognize the Bible is not raw material waiting for theology to happen. It is already theology." He concludes his article with: "We are beckoned to live this story, to inhabit the narrative of God's ongoing and gracious purpose for the world—so we resist attempting to revise the words of scripture to make them match our reality. Instead, we must make sense of our reality, our lives, within the scripture's story. Embracing the Bible as scripture, we do not accept it as one narrative among others, but accord it a privilege above all others, and allow ourselves to be shaped by it."

Professor Green critiques what he refers to as "linear hermeneutics"—the rational process of linguistic and historical analysis of the biblical texts, identification of common ideas in the canon, and articulation of timeless doctrinal principles. Although not disparaging the contribution of historical-critical methods as a corrective to an assumed identity of church dogma with the message of the Bible, he pleads for a dynamic relationship of Bible and theology with focus on shaping and nurturing the faith and life of God's people. "As the instrument of revelation, scripture presents the paradigm by which Christians make sense of the world in relation to God; it is therefore incumbent on Christians to engage in theological reflection on scripture whereby their imaginations are yielded to its theological vision. This practice will not overcome the problems of diversity of perspectives within the Bible, but it will focus our imaginative faculties on the pattern of the story (or 'plot') that runs from creation to the new creation, with the Christ-event as its interpretive middle—or to shift the metaphor, on the 'voice' of scripture heard as a choir of voices engaged in melody and counter-melody." [1]

Third, we must look at specific rules related to marriage. (These include whom to marry, determination of virginity, rape, adultery, arrangements for childless widows, and marital specifications for priests and elders.) Some of these reflect and arise out of the cultural setting of the covenant people at a given time. This leaves us with the task of determining what weight they have in the big picture.

Fourth, we must examine some highly relevant texts (Old Testament and New Testament). Those with theological implications are of particular interest. How the New Testament uses Old Testament texts is especially enlightening.

Finally, we must compare biblical accounts with the views and practices of surrounding cultures. This aspect of the research calls for paying close attention to commonalities with the surrounding cultures and the significant differences stemming from a different faith and worldview.

A theology of marriage needs to go beyond analysis of the biblical material to a synthesis of the theological strands emerging from the whole of God's revelation (written and in the person of Christ). It aims to

1. Green, "Scripture and Theology," 18–20.

ascertain the big picture and avoid building a case on selected texts. The imagery for this endeavor is interesting. To speak of finding clues implies that we are trying to solve a puzzle or mystery. To speak of distilling suggests a boiling down of evidence or of collecting the most-volatile parts, or perhaps the least-volatile parts. Even identifying the process as synthesis runs the risk of leaving the impression that the result is "synthetic," with connotations of being artificially contrived. Despite the inherent hazards, the present confusion makes discernment of a biblically based theology of marriage imperative.

Two more related factors regarding the biblical material need to be taken into account. One has to do with what is assumed without specifically saying it. The Bible reports marriage as nearly universal in practice (especially in the Old Testament), assuming it to be normative without specific injunctions. Likewise, it assumes marriage to be a male-female relationship, again without explicitly saying so. The other factor, which is closely related, is the element of silence. Arguments from silence are risky at best. But in this case, because of the nature of the material, a biblical theology must draw some deductions from what is assumed, implied, only indirectly addressed, and not said at all. Those deductions are then to be tested by how they mesh with Scripture as a whole.

We are not dealing with a "flat Bible." Texts out of context will not carry the freight of a theology of the kind we need in the malaise of marriage and family questions and challenges today. There are internal tensions in the biblical canon. In those cases we need to discern where the weight, the center, is in biblical revelation and not play what has been called "proof text poker." The subjective elements of discernment must be tested for integrity. It is all too easy to slip into finding what one wants to find or to read the Bible out of a given family experience, reacting to particular weaknesses in one's family of origin. Notions of the "ideal" family vary widely and are too easily read back into the biblical data. In chapter 3 of *From Culture Wars to Common Ground,* Don S. Browning describes the differences in North American traditions in colonial Puritan families in the Northeast, southern slave and slave-holding families, Native American matrilineal families, Victorian families in the Midwest and the southern frontier, Roman Catholicism in the Southwest, and the influences of enlightenment and evangelicalism.

The difficulties of the search are real. Yet the faith presuppositions remain that there is a "word from the Lord" for our time and that it will be found to be consonant with the written word and what God has spoken through his Son. This study contributes seminal factors out of which a biblical theology of marriage is built. Please note that this book does not pretend to be a biblical theology of marriage in the strict definition of biblical theology. It does aim to call attention to significant "from the ground up" biblical data arising out the vocabulary study, data that is foundational in discerning what the Bible has to say about marriage.

C. METHODS EMPLOYED

After a survey of what has and has not been done in delineating a theology of marriage, I gave primary attention to the vocabulary employed in the biblical languages. This included noting root meanings, usage, multiple meanings, nuances, and word combinations in all Hebrew and Greek words associated with marriage in the Old Testament and New Testament. In many cases both noun and verb forms were included (plus several adjectival forms), resulting in well over one hundred Hebrew and Greek words deemed relevant to the study. (See the vocabulary lists in the appendix.) The Septuagint (LXX) provides linkages for how the New Testament uses the Old Testament and also adds a few Greek words not used in the New Testament. Beyond the several words for husband and for wife, the pertinent vocabulary included terms for engagement, bride and bridegroom, marry/marriage, concubine, adultery, divorce, references to love and sex in marriage, and other terms arising in key texts that reveal understandings about marriage. The relevant words are about equally divided between Hebrew and Greek. Useful reference sources included concordances, lexicons, and dictionaries.

Vocabulary studies reveal several notable features of the way the Bible speaks of marriage. These will be highlighted in the compilation of findings that follows (notably in chapter 3, section B.1). More extensive notes on the vocabulary research are found in the appendix. Certain texts throughout the canon deserve more intense study to discern their contribution to the theological construct. These are also noted in the findings. Library facilities enabled my effort to become acquainted with scholarly books and articles pertinent to the issue (especially what has come out of the last several decades). Since northeastern Ohio does not have a theological library, I did research in Asbury Theological Seminary Library, Ashland Theological Seminary Library, Associated Mennonite Biblical

Seminary Library, and Pittsburgh Theological Seminary Library, as well as at Youngstown State University Library. Internet resources are almost unlimited!

Two Pastor Peer Groups have afforded settings for engaging other students of the Bible in exploring the biblical material and in evaluating the emerging affirmations. In an effort to avoid overlooking some texts and for testing conclusions, I have consulted several skilled scholars throughout the search and writing. Several peers have read the manuscript drafts along the way and have shared encouragement and insightful suggestions. The affirmations extended by the Swiss Reformed pastor are encouraging. Insights arising out of his study prompted expansion of several themes. These will be noted in context. The bibliography lists sources quoted or referred to and other sources consulted in the research.

3

Overview of the Biblical Data

THE FINDINGS OF THE study in this part of the book are in this format: a concise statement in italic type, followed by elaboration, noting what led to each affirmation.

A. PRELIMINARY OBSERVATIONS

1. Three Frames

The biblical material falls into three fairly distinct frames: Genesis 1–2, Genesis 3–Malachi, and the New Testament.

Genesis 1 and 2 constitute the pre-fall frame ("Eden"), which includes two somewhat different accounts pertaining to marriage. The rest of the Old Testament reflects marriage and related sexuality practices, revealing God's intent being lived out, some movements away from the original plan and provision, and some degree of return later to intended norms. In this middle period, human marriage is seen as an analogy of the covenant relationship between Yahweh and his people. The New Testament addresses the deviations, compromises, and double standards evidenced in the Old Testament story. Jesus and Paul both reach back to the pre-fall accounts (Gen 1–2). This means that a biblical theology of marriage must be built on the foundation in the creation accounts and then be expanded by the redemption perspective of the New Testament.

The big picture, theologically speaking, needs to include also the eschatological reference to the marriage of the Lamb. Biblical revelation ends with the imagery of a marriage supper for Christ (the Lamb) and his bride/wife (the faithful). The framing of the canon with the marriage imagery, even though Jesus said there is no marriage in heaven, elevates human marriage far beyond congeniality and convenience, as we will see.

The Old Testament frames are not as neatly defined when the times of writing/compilation are taken into account. The immediate contexts no doubt shaped what was included or not included, even if we do not go as far as finding revisions and alterations. As noted earlier, silence about a particular marriage issue does not necessarily mean it was not important. It may have been assumed to being the ongoing norm. However, as referenced in the New Testament, the first frame offers an identifiable perspective on how things were at the beginning, and how they are intended to be.

2. Male and Female in the Image of God

Male and female are created in the image of God and given a shared assignment.

The special creation account in Genesis 1:26–28 provides no specific reference to marriage. The focus is on male and female being created in the image of God, blessed, and charged with exercising dominion over the created animal order and with multiplying. The implication is that it is male and female together in relationship that reflect the image of God. However, the relational aspect dare not be pushed to the point that single persons are not understood to be in the image of God (e.g., Jesus, Paul, and all others). Yet personhood is experienced in community, including inter-gender relationships. The fact that the assignment includes procreation supports the perception that it is male and female together that is in view in this text, with overtones of marriage, although not explicitly worded that way. We should observe in this text that no division of labor (between male and female) is specified in the assignment to be fruitful, multiply, subdue, and have dominion. It reads as a shared human responsibility, without specifying that females are to be fruitful and males to exercise dominion.

The fact that exercising dominion follows immediately after being made in the image and likeness of God (*Elohim*) suggests there is a relationship between these two specifications. Although the translations commonly use the connective "and," the Hebrew *vav* could be construed as a coordinating conjunction rather than a subordinating conjunction, with the sense of "so that."[1] That is, human beings (as male and female) are

---

1. Towner, "Clones of God," 248.

able to fulfill their management assignment because of their being made in the divine image. It follows that they are to carry out their vocation in ways consistent with the way the Creator exercises dominion. Genesis 1:26–28 gives human relationships a three-dimensional thrust: with the Creator, with each other (the fellowship of male and female), and with the charges of their stewardship and management.

A special act of creation and the double reference to "image of God" establishes that the human male and female are more closely linked to the Creator than to the lower animal kingdom (although there are biological similarities). In Hebrew, "image" is *tselem* (Gen 1:26–27; 5:1; 9:6). In the LXX it is *eikōn* (also of Christ in Col 1:15). "Likeness" is a synonymous term, emphasizing the divine-human connection. In Hebrew it is *dmut*, and in the LXX *homoiōsis* (also in the same sense in Jas 3:9).

When we respect the literary structure of Genesis 1, we see the creative action moving from "Let there be . . . Let the waters . . . Let the earth . . ." to "Let us make . . ." This plus the triple "created" in verse 27 sets humankind apart from the rest of the created order. Human beings are made "a little lower than God" (as the Hebrew reads in Ps 8:5), not a little higher than the other creatures. The reference to "male and female" occurs regarding humans in Genesis 1 and 2 but not in reference to the non-human animals. Therefore more is implied than biological capability to reproduce. Being made as male and female in the image of God and in relationship with each other is what the term "sexuality" encompasses.

Considerable debate revolves around how to understand "in the image of God." Karl Barth, in his extensive discussion of *imago dei* (*Church Dogmatics, III*), argued that to be in the image of God is to be male and female. Although allowing for wider application than marriage, Barth's reading of Genesis 1 as primarily focusing on marriage comes close to excluding singles from participating in the image of God. The term "cohumanity," as descriptive of the interrelationship of male and female in God's image, does apply to both the married and the unmarried. Another way to say it is that the image of God "consists in that difference-in-likeness, or likeness-in-difference that marks all humans."[2] We are left wondering how the "image" applies to both the male-female pair and individual humans. Howard Charles comments, "Both maleness and femaleness as such may be essential in some profound and mysterious way to the full embodi-

---

2. Finger, *Christian Theology,* 106.

ment of the divine image."[3] (Views of singleness in the biblical data will be explored later, in chapter 5, section B.5.)

Whether or not marriage is read into the text, the wording implies equality, mutuality, and shared responsibility for the male and female. Male and female together are constituted for interacting and working together (within and apart from marriage and sex), as well as communing and working with and representing God. Although the commandment to honor father and mother is frequently listed in the second table of the Decalogue, it rightly fits with the first table, in the sense of showing respect for representatives of Yahweh, along with respecting his name and consecrated day.

The two creation accounts, although commonly designated as Genesis 1 and Genesis 2, divide as 1:1—2:3 and 2:4–25 and not according to the chapter division imposed on the text. Both accounts are in narrative rather than propositional form, with different but complementary structures. The first account ascends from elemental creation to the making of humankind. The second quickly focuses on the forming of the human element of creation. As Howard H. Charles has put it, "In chapter 1 the human pair is the pinnacle of a pyramid, while in chapter 2 they are the center of a circle."[4] One attempt to reduce the difference and tension between Genesis 1 and 2 has been the notion that the first human was androgynous (bisexual), later to be separated into two (man and woman). This "solution" draws on mythology rather than biblical revelation. The imposed supposition that Genesis 1 and 2 are in strict chronological sequence raises more problems than the androgynous idea solves. It is better to take the separate creation accounts as reflecting different perspectives of God's creative actions.

The language of "image" and "likeness" does not support the reverse argument that God must therefore have physical features and sexuality like humans. "Likeness" occurs again in Genesis 5:1. As the story unfolds, we see that humans are enough like God to enable communication and spiritual communion. As someone has put it, "We are made with a capacity to think God's thoughts after him." Colossians 1:15, Jesus's claims (e.g., John 14:9–11), and Hebrews 1:1–3 add the element of representation to

---

3. Charles, *Opening the Bible*, 77.

4. Ibid., 75.

an understanding of Christ as image, an element that is true to a degree in the design for all humankind.

In contrast with the surrounding pagan cultures, God's revelation to the Hebrews does not connect human fertility to sexual activity between the gods and goddesses. Reproductive ability (fecundity) is an endowment from the Creator, not to be acquired through sensuous fertility rites.

The Bible seems to assume that what constitutes maleness and what constitutes femaleness does not need precise definition. It seems to take for granted that the male and female are different but provides no identifiable distinction, other than obvious anatomical differences in genitalia and reproduction. Characteristics such as bisexualism, hermaphroditism, and transvestitism are not evident in the biblical accounts. However, same-gender attractions and sexual activities are reported and spoken to.

3. Covenant Partners

The man and his counterpart, the newly formed woman, have a social/ spiritual/sexual unity as covenant partners, expressed as "one flesh." This primary expression of community is God's solution to an otherwise incompleteness and loneliness.

Genesis 2:18–25 implies a marriage relationship, although that term is not used here either. To "become one flesh" implies sexual union, although the Genesis 2 passage does not at all mention fertility or reproduction (as is true in Gen 1). From a New Testament perspective "one flesh," known by the theological term *henosis*, means much more than physical union, as will be explored later (in chapter 4, section A).

The remedy for what was "not good" (being alone) includes the discovery that the animal kingdom does not provide any being that corresponds to and is a counterpart for the man. The wording "suitable helper" (TNIV) conveys the sense of complementarity. Since the term helper, *ezer*, is most frequently used in the Bible of God, it in no way connotes inferiority or second-class status. A relationship of both continuity and discontinuity stems from woman being specially built "out of" the man, yet different and not a clone. It follows from the resultant polarity that neither is complete alone.

The leaving and cleaving in 2:24, better expressed as separating from and attaching to, uses covenant language to assert the priority of marriage over parental family ties. Although not to be pushed to require a complete

disjunction with the family of origin, the new social entity entails a fundamental change in primary relationships. A footnote in Brenton's English
translation of the LXX suggests "be cemented" for "cleave."

The components of marriage in Genesis 2 are basic to an understanding of marriage in God's design. Alongside the focus on marriage,
it needs to be noted that the human need for intimacy and friendship
is met in part in same-gender relationships. In the Creator's design, the
complementarity of male and female is also experienced apart from marriage and sex.

Regarding the contention that naming symbolizes "power over" in
Genesis 2:23, greater significance should be seen in *what* he named her
than in *that* he named her. Although we might expect the name to be the
feminine form of *adam*, which would be *adamah* (the word for ground),
we find the man, *ish*, calling her woman, *ishah*. This pair of words is also
common for husband and wife. In *Sketches of Jewish Social Life in the
Days of Christ*, Alfred Edersheim notes "that even the Hebrew name for
'woman,' given her at her creation (Gen ii.23), marked a wife as a companion of her husband, and his equal ('Ishah,' a woman, from 'Ish,' a man)."[5]
(More on this language peculiarity later.)

The expression "bone of my bones and flesh of my flesh" carries
several meanings. Bone connotes power, and flesh connotes weakness.
Although antithetical, they come together so that both the man and the
woman share in the whole picture of humanness. The bone-flesh expression expands in meaning in the Old Testament from blood relative to
covenant loyalty apart from blood relationship. In Genesis 2, the imagery
expresses a strong bond.

Verse 23 ends the words of the man, addressed to God (not the
woman). Verse 24 is the comment of the author/editor, reflecting a later
perspective. The original pair did not have father and mother to leave!
Why this text refers only to the husband leaving the parental home is
not at all clear. It may reflect social factors at the time of writing, which
perhaps assumed that the wife leaves her home and intentionally specifies
that husbands are to do likewise. Some commentators, such as Keil and
Delitzsch, take the rule to apply equally to both marital partners.[6]

---

5. Edersheim, *Sketches of Jewish Social Life*, 98.

6. Keil and Delitzsch, *Commentaries*, 90.

The man's separation in order to be attached to the woman, rather than the other way around, could suggest a matriarchal orientation. The Old Testament accounts include limited evidence of matriarchy (*sadiqa*). In Genesis 24:28, Rebekah runs to tell her mother's household about the arrival of Abraham's servant. A practice known as *beena* is one in which the husband settles in the wife's house, with the children under the mother's control (Jacob and Moses are examples of this). In a *mota* arrangement, the wife stays with kin and the husband visits (as with Timnah and Samson).[7]

Translations are not at all uniform as to where in the Genesis accounts the proper name Adam is used first, and the translation variations can be confusing. The Hebrew word *adam*, with and without an article attached, shifts in meaning from "humankind" or "man" in a generic sense to "the man" and eventually to "Adam" (at least by Gen 4:25).

4. Jesus and Genesis 1 and 2

Jesus shows us how to read Genesis 1 and 2, integrating the two accounts relevant to marriage and reinforcing them with additional explanation and directives. In Jesus's teaching, marriage is two (a male and a female) becoming one, with God involved in the joining.

Matthew 19:3–9 and Mark 10:2–12 both have Jesus responding to a question about divorce, a question intended to trap him. (Jesus's teaching about divorce will be noted in chapter 6, section A.2.) His response has direct quotations from Genesis 1 and 2 imbedded in it, quotations that basically follow the LXX (as do most Old Testament quotations found in the New Testament). Jesus focuses on marriage (rather than divorce), noting how it was "at the beginning" (Matt 19:4), "from the beginning of creation" (Mark 10:6). He runs together wording from Genesis 1:27, "Made them male and female," and 2:24, "For this reason a man shall leave his father and his mother and be joined to his wife, and the two shall become one flesh" (Matt 19:5). Jesus connects these texts as if Genesis 2:24 follows from 1:27. Jesus ignores the fact that Genesis 2:24 is not the words of the man, as in 2:23, but rather an editorial comment. Jesus considered it all of equal weight. Jesus quotes these texts as specifying divine intent from the beginning, even though scholarly opinion does not hold Genesis to be the first of written revelation.

---

7. Baab, "Marriage," 279.

A close comparison of the Hebrew and Greek (LXX) of Genesis 1:27 and of 2:24 reveals almost identical construction and word order, even though one language is Semitic and the other is Indo-European. It appears as though the translators of the LXX retained as much of the literary details of these texts as is possible across diverse languages, thus suggesting their high regard for these fundamental statements. Jesus quoting from them increases their weight.

Although the accounts in Genesis 1 and 2 viewed separately each contribute to an understanding of marriage, by combining them Jesus unmistakably connects male and female to marriage. His added comment, "So they are no longer two, but one flesh," reinforces the point. God's involvement, expressed as "what God has joined together" (Matt 19:6; Mark 10:9) would seem to go beyond having created male and female with an "urge to merge."

The aorist verb *synezeuxev* (in Matt 19 and Mark 10), translated as "joined together," has the sense of being yoked together, as a team. The vernacular expression, "getting hitched," thus has textual/theological support.

Martin Luther understood that prior to the disobedience in Genesis 3, the man and woman were "equal in all respects," and that subordination and domination came into their relationship as a result of their disobedience. John Calvin, however, understood that the initial relationship was what might be called "benevolent subordination," in line with the way he understood 1 Corinthians 11 in hierarchical terms.[8] As Eugene F. Ropp notes, the church has tended to be more in touch with Calvin than with Luther on this matter. But as we have seen earlier, the wording in Genesis 1 and 2 and the way Jesus connected the two passages do not support hierarchy in the beginning.

The accounts in Matthew 19:3–9 and Mark 10:2–12 are not identical reports. They do not quote the LXX of Genesis 2:24 exactly the same, and neither of them is exactly like the LXX as we have it today. The differences are minor, and the fact that the two accounts are not identical increases their value, since they convey essentially the same teaching from two editorial perspectives. The Masoretic text does not have "two" in Genesis 2:24 (as do the LXX and the New Testament quotations), but the Samaritan version does include it.

8. Ropp, *Genesis*, 323.

Proverbs 19:14 in the LXX has "a wife is suited to (*harmozō*) a man by the Lord." In 2 Corinthians 11:2, the same verb conveys that the apostle betrothed believers to Christ, as a virgin is promised to one husband. Malachi 2:13–14 says the reason Yahweh is not accepting offerings is "because the Lord was a witness between you and the wife of your youth, to whom you have been faithless, though she is your companion and your wife by covenant." Although we find no specific biblical evidence of marriage ceremonies evoking Yahweh's blessing, the silence does not rule out God being consciously included in the family formalities. These several texts and the solemn covenant nature of marriage imply that God at least took note of the marriage and held the couple accountable, whether actually mentioned in the ceremonies or not.

When Jesus was asked a loaded question about divorce (Matt 19:3; Mark 10:2), he directed attention to marriage as it was in the beginning. If Jesus were asked if same-gender couples should not also be given the benefit of formal marriage, might he not also first go to the fundamental texts about marriage, converging Genesis 1:27–28 and 2:24? What is revealed about the Creator's design and intent for marriage should be the framework for considering questions of the parameters of marriage.

B. BIBLICAL VOCABULARY OF MARRIAGE

As noted in the earlier section on methods employed in this study, the biblical vocabulary associated with marriage received primary attention. The larger picture entails much more than the primary words, such as marriage, marry, wife, and husband. In the main part of this treatise the Hebrew and Greek words are in transliteration form. The full list (Hebrew and Greek words with English transliterations), with brief notations of meaning, is in the appendix. When words have more than one meaning, the associations can help in sensing what they add to an understanding of marriage. General observations follow, with more detailed notes on vocabulary in the appendix.

1. Vocabulary Reflects Practice and Culture

Much of the vocabulary used to speak of marriage partners and the marriage relationship reflects the practice of marriage in the culture of the time, along with indications of divine intent.

Observations on Hebrew Vocabulary

Some of the vocabulary reveals that wives were considered to be the property of men. To marry was to acquire a wife. Daughters were characteristically viewed as the possession of fathers, who gave their daughters in marriage and who took wives for their sons (e.g., Jer 29:6). The tenth commandment (Exod 20:17) prohibits coveting a neighbor's wife along with his house, slaves, animals, or anything else that belongs to the neighbor. However, even though it was predominantly a man's world, wives were not in the same category as chattel. They were not to be sold. In fact, alongside the words connoting ownership, we find terms indicating companionship, living with each other responsibly, a sense of being a team, and expressions of tenderness and sometimes mutuality. There certainly were good, fulfilling marriages in Old Testament times.

A sexual component of marriage is implicit in several words. (The accompanying drive to produce children will be noted later.) The term marriage tends to focus on a wedding with an attending celebration, all in a family context.

Engagement required the consent of both sets of parents. Marriage was a family event. Although marriage created a new and distinct social unit (as noted in connection with Gen 2:24), it entailed not only marrying an individual but also marrying into a family. Eloping and getting married privately was apparently inconceivable in any of the Old Testament cultures.

Many of the words indicating human marriage are also used to identify the relationship of God and his chosen people. This analogy served to help humans, who knew marriage experientially, to understand their covenant relationship with Yahweh, especially the effects of their unfaithfulness. From our distance and understanding of God's covenants, the analogy sheds light on the intent for human marriage.

Observations on the LXX (Greek Old Testament) Vocabulary

The transcultural shift from Hebrew to Greek could be expected to utilize some different thought forms (even though the translators were Hebrews, albeit Hellenized), and such is the case. A few nuances of meaning emerge in the choice of Greek words, but the overall picture of marriage parallels what we find in the Hebrew Old Testament. The vocabulary reflects attitudes ranging from male dominance to complementarity. The most significant change is in the emergence of *agapē* as the primary translation of the Hebrew word for love, *ahab*. (See the elaboration in chapter 4, section C.)

OBSERVATIONS ON NEW TESTAMENT GREEK VOCABULARY

Compared with the Hebrew and Greek Old Testament (LXX), the New Testament vocabulary itself produces few surprises. Marriage continues to be thought of in most instances as the wedding rather than the ongoing marital relationship. The assumption that marriage is for one male and one female continues. One notable change is in the bridegroom being used in reference to Christ (rather than to Yahweh, as in the Old Testament). Another is the recognition of singleness as equally acceptable, growing out of a changing view of the value of posterity.

Several significant changes that are not directly tied to the vocabulary involved (e.g., removal of the double standard with respect to adultery) are treated separately.

2. Man-husband, Woman-wife

In both Hebrew (Old Testament) and Greek (LXX and New Testament), the most common word for man is also the most common word for husband; and the most common word for woman is also the most common word for wife. This phenomenon in both languages cannot be counted as coincidental.

The primary Hebrew word for an individual male and for husband is *ish*. It is used in the human husband-wife relationship and of God in relationship to his people (Hos 2:16).

The primary Hebrew word for woman and for wife is *ishah*. By analogy Israel is depicted as the wife of Yahweh (Jer 3:1; Ezek 16:32). This word has broad connotations: from high regard to possession, from wise to foolish, from mother to whore.

The primary Greek word for both man and husband is *anēr*. It is used of God as a husband in the LXX and of Christ as the husband of believers (2 Cor 11:2).

The primary Greek word for woman and wife is *gynē*, and it is also used for bride and widow. As with its counterpart, it is used of the covenant people as the wife of Yahweh (LXX of Ezek 16:32). This is as close as the Bible comes to picturing God as having a wife, although the pagan deities of the time had their female counterparts.

The fact that this phenomenon occurs in both Hebrew and Greek, languages from two vastly differing language families (Semitic and Indo-European), elevates it above a localized linguistic fluke. The two languages are vehicles of highly dissimilar cultures, evident in thought patterns and worldviews. Upon first learning of this vocabulary phenomenon, one might wonder if this is implying that to be truly a man one must be married and that to be truly a woman one must be married. That takes the linguistic factor too far. The primary explanation of this phenomenon may well be that in both cultures it was assumed that a man would become a husband and that a woman would become a wife. That is, marriage was understood to be the norm. Yet as these two distinct languages are overlaid in the Scriptures, this particular similarity seems also to reinforce the norm in biblical revelation that a husband is a man and a wife is a woman.

In all four of these words, it is sometimes a translator's choice whether to render as man or husband, woman or wife. (See analysis of 1 Cor 11:3–16 in chapter 5, section B.6.) If a possessive pronoun is attached, a marital relationship may be implied, but it is not always that simple.

In both Hebrew (Old Testament) and Greek (LXX and New Testament), the several other nouns used for husband and for wife (and related words, such as bridegroom and bride) are also all gender consistent. The languages themselves accord with the assumption that a husband is a male and a wife is a female.

Several nouns occur in both masculine and feminine forms, sometimes with slightly different connotations. One exception is with the masculine noun *adam*, translated as the name Adam and as man, carrying a generic sense (human, humankind). But note that this has to do with *adam*, not with *ish*, and thus does not alter the rule of gender consistency. Similarly, the LXX renders the generic sense of *adam* as *anthrōpos*, also generic, although commonly translated as "man."

4

Weighty Words and Concepts

A. ONE FLESH—*HENOSIS*

IN TEACHINGS ABOUT MARRIAGE, both Jesus and Paul pick up on a term emerging first in Genesis 2:24, becoming "one flesh." This summary expression for marriage implies sexual union, plus much more of what marriage in the Creator's design encompasses.

In Hebrew, the term is *basar ekhad,* combining "flesh" as a way of expressing the totality of being a person with the much-used word and concept of unity, "one." In Greek (New Testament) the wording is *mia sarx* (found in Matt 19:5–6; Mark 10:8; 1 Cor 6:16; Eph 5:31).

As in Hebrew, the English word "flesh" connotes more than the physical body, and "one" conveys an existential unity. The theological term *henosis,* from the same word family as the Greek word *mia,* has come into usage as applied to the unity/oneness at the heart of marriage. It is not a New Testament word but was used by Ignatius (early second century) and means marriage.[1] It is a good word and concept, reminding us that "going our separate ways together" falls far short of God's intent for marriage.

Jesus, when confronted with questions about divorce, redirected the focus to marriage and cited Genesis 1:27 and 2:24. Jesus is saying that clearly understanding the core nature of the marriage bond must come before getting into arguments about procedures for ending a marriage. Division must be seen in reference to the God-ordained unity of two, male and female, becoming one flesh. (Jesus's teaching on divorce comes up later.)

---

1. Ignatius to Polycarp, 5:2, in Lake, *Apostolic Fathers.*

In 1 Corinthians 6:12–20, Paul counters the libertine view that what one does with the body has no effect on spirituality, specifically that coitus with a prostitute does not matter. To expose the fallacy of libertine thinking that sex is only a physical act, he cites Genesis 2:24, specifically the line, "The two will become one flesh." In this pericope, Paul does not mention marriage, but by including a quotation from Genesis 2:24, a fundamental text on marriage, Paul goes on to say categorically that fornication violates union with Christ. He thus puts Christ into the "one flesh" equation. Key words include: Lord/Christ, body, member of, united to, one, spirit, and fornication/prostitute (both from the Greek word *porneia*). Both "body" and "one flesh" call for a closer look.

In 1 Corinthians 6:16, body (*sōma*) and flesh (*sarx*) appear almost interchangeable. For the most part, both terms identify the whole person and not just the physical aspect of human existence.[2] The central issue in Paul's rejoinder to the libertine position is the view of the body. According to this view, if the human body is only a physical entity, then sex, even illicit sex, is no different from eating a sandwich to satisfy an empty stomach. Paul disagrees adamantly with that line of reasoning. Our bodies belong to the Lord by virtue of creation and redemption, to which Paul adds resurrection to come and being temples of the Holy Spirit. It could be argued that other activities besides fornication also desecrate the body-temple. But Paul's point is that sex outside of marriage violates union with Christ. The sex act (expressed as "knowing" in Hebrew and Greek) uniquely bonds the partners as bodies, as persons. Paul goes so far as to say that the oneness of the believer with Christ is analogous to the "one flesh" of marriage.

Is the first act of coitus unique in terms of "one flesh"? Has the first-hand "knowledge" line has been crossed? Few are prepared to say that the first sexual encounter results in a binding "one flesh," but certainly experimental/recreational sex has more implications than young people, or people of any age, realize.

The relevance of this passage for a biblical understanding of marriage is in what is implied. Paul asserts pointedly that illicit sex—sex outside of marriage—is incompatible with a believer's union with Christ. The important flip-side is that marital union not only does not violate union with Christ but is also consonant with oneness with Christ.

2. See Schweizer and Baumgärtel, "σάρξ," and "σῶμα," for extensive discussion of the relationship of these two terms.

Ephesians 5:31 echoes the root text about "one flesh" (Gen 2:24) and does so in a framework that magnifies *Christ* and *love*. The frequency and distribution of these two key words establish the connection between Christ-church oneness and human marriage. Six times in the Greek text we find *Christ* (*Christos*) and six times *love* (*agapē*). In this expanded part of the Household Codes,[3] according to Ephesians, the primary focus is on Christ and the church (mentioned five times), with specific application to the husband-wife relationship. The result is a christological concept of marriage. Here Christology and human marriage intersect for the purpose of shaping and informing the basic human social unit as God intends it to be. In his treatment of Ephesians 5, Marcus Barth comments: "A greater, wiser, and more positive description of marriage has not yet been found in Christian literature."[4]

Several details of Ephesians 5:21–33 call for comment. The word *hupotassomenoi* in verse 21, commonly translated as "submit" or "be subject," is the fifth of a series of participles in verses 19–21, connecting it with verses 15–20. Participles are sometimes construed as imperatives, but here they most naturally stand as true participles, following the imperative "be filled" in verse 18. Whether a comma is appropriate after verse 20 or after verse 21, verse 21 is a bridge, because verse 22 does not have the participle repeated (as most translations imply). The call to mutual subordination in verse 21, implied in verse 22, is in present middle form, indicating voluntary action (submit yourself). As to the motive, "in the fear of Christ," *phobos* in verse 21 needs to inform how we understand "fear" in verse 33. The NRSV has "reverence" in verse 21 and "respect" in verse 33. "Due respect" could serve in both verses. The word to husbands, love your wives (vv. 25 and 33), is an imperative. The summary word to the wife (v. 33) is a subjunctive, "should show due respect," slightly less direct.

The amount of words/space addressed to husbands, compared with that to wives, suggests who most needed to hear and apply the Christ-church analogy. The comparison of the Christ-church and husband-wife

---

3. The term Household Code(s) designates a genre of New Testament ethical teaching found primarily in Colossians 3:18—4:1, Ephesians 5:21—6:9, and 1 Peter 2:13—3:7 (with a different format). Luther used the term *Haustafeln* for these teachings addressed to the counterparts of the household (husbands—wives, fathers—children, and masters—slaves). They come into the marriage picture because of the hierarchical relationship that seems to be implied.

4. Barth, *Ephesians 4-6*, 715.

relationships is not entirely parallel, of course, (e.g., Christ as Savior). However, the analogy must be fully respected because it is the point of the passage. What Christ does as head of the church tells us what headship means for husbands. The emphasis is on love and fulfillment. (More on the Household Codes in chapter 7, section C.)

Common translations of verses 28–30 leave the impression that a man's innate self-love is the primary basis for loving a wife. Marcus Barth goes as far as to say that a rendering with that impression is "ambiguous, inaccurate and contrary to the intent of the context."[5] Barth calls us to recognize the parallel between Christ and his body (the church), and a husband and his body (meaning his wife). The flow of the context is not from a husband's self-love to love of his wife, but from Christ's love of his body to a husband's love of his wife, and then to loving himself in loving his wife. Connecting the first phrase of verse 28 to what is in the previous verses, Barth offers the translation: "In the same manner also husbands owe it [to God and man] to love their wives for they are their bodies."[6] It follows that because she is his body/flesh (they have become "one flesh"), he will love, provide for, and care for her. The spring of action for the love of the husband for his wife is the love of Christ for his body, the church.

This careful reading of the text is crucial in recognizing the christological construct of marriage. Barth's exegesis of Ephesians 5:21–33 leads him to conclude: "The Christ-church union is not one feature among others which give the marital union its ground, validity, form, purpose, and blessing: in Eph 5, it is the sole basis upon which all statements on marriage are founded."[7]

Barth's careful exegesis does not lend support to taking "love your neighbor as you love yourself" as the basis for an equal-regard marriage relationship. However, it does support the perspective that surfaces in the next section that agape love focuses more on giving than on getting, including the marriage relationship.

Unquestionably, Ephesians 5:31 is a quotation of Genesis 2:24, closer to the LXX than to the Hebrew. Minor differences suggest that either there was more than one edition of the LXX around or it was being quoted from

---

5. Ibid., 629.

6. Ibid.

7. Ibid., 737.

memory. Some text sources add "of his flesh and of his bones," included in Textus Receptus and KJV.

Although the expression "two become one flesh" may for many convey little more than physical union, biblical usage gives it the sense of bonding that potentially involves the whole personhood of each one. The goal of marital union is not to eradicate individual personhood. Rather, it becomes the setting for sanctifying each other in becoming what each is created and gifted to be and do. Particularly, as this union draws on the Christ-church union, Ephesians 5 opens vistas of experience in marriage. And it opens an opportunity and challenge to let marital life give witness to the wonder of Christ and his bride.

B. COVENANT

Marriage arises out of the created order as a mutual covenant relationship, sustained by fidelity and love, with God's covenant with his people as the prototype.

Marriage is a near-universal practice shaped by natural law irrespective of direct knowledge and worship of Yahweh. In biblical revelation, the Creator-Redeemer's intent for human marriage between male and female is that it be informed by and mirror the divine-human covenant as most fully experienced in Jesus Christ. This is to say, those who know experientially the "new covenant" in Christ have not only a heightened view of their marriage as a covenant relationship; they also have an inner incentive to exercise grace and forgiveness toward each other, as an extension of the forgiveness provided in the new covenant (e.g., Jer 31:31–34, and as quoted in Heb 8). The bar is higher, and the enablement to live up to the potential is a given, as appropriated.

Characterizing marriage as a covenant construct elevates it above simply a relationship or even a contract. Viewed as covenant, marriage takes on elements of mutuality, holy seriousness, obligations as well as promises, no refunds or provisions for backing out, and accountability not only to each other but also to the witnessing God. Human marriage entails multiple covenants—the marriage partners with each other, their covenant before God, and the mutual covenant with extended family, witnesses, and the spiritual community in which they should be active.

Covenants as binding commitments served in the ancient world to define relationships between sovereign states, between overlords and vassals, and between individuals. Old Testament examples include: Abraham and Abimelech (Gen 21:25–32) and Jacob and Laban (Gen 31:44–54). Covenants were often confirmed with oaths and symbolic signs, and perhaps calling on God as witness (1 Sam 23:18). Yahweh's covenant with the chosen people became the prime example.

The Bible recognizes two kinds of covenants. Covenants of parity are between persons who are equals who enter into a mutual covenant. Covenants of suzerainty are between unequals—as between feudal lords and their subjects and between God and his people. Some of God's covenants are conditional, and some are unconditional/unilateral. The parallel between human marriage and Yahweh's "marriage" with his chosen people could be construed as human marriage also being designed as between unequals, a covenant of suzerainty. Does the evidence support this seemingly logical deduction?

Some of the vocabulary of the Old Testament, reflecting a male-dominated society, expresses marriage as a man taking/acquiring a wife. The connotation is not that of parity. There are, however, evidences of the female's consent being sought, although women captured as slaves were not in a position to make a choice about marriage. Ruth is an example of the female exercising initiative in becoming married to Boaz. As we will see, Malachi 2 charges husbands with violating their marriage covenant with the wives of their youth in order to marry foreign women. In Proverbs 2:17, the seductive, adulterous woman who forsakes the partner of her youth is charged with forgetting her sacred covenant. At least to some extent human marriage was understood to be a mutual, voluntary commitment or covenant in the Old Testament. God holds married couples accountable to their covenants with each other as part of their covenant responsibility to God. The New Testament provides increasing evidence of marriage being a mutual commitment, pointing to it being a covenant of parity. Later we will explore the authority factor in 1 Corinthians 7.

An array of texts from Genesis to Malachi place marriage in the genre of covenant, even though the term itself is seldom used. In Genesis 2:23, the wording "bone of my bones and flesh of my flesh" has covenant overtones. (In Gen 29:14, this expression is used of blood relatives; in Judg 9:2, it means clan or kinfolk; in 2 Sam 5:1, it describes the relationship of the tribes to David—cousins plus covenant commitment; in 1 Chr 11:1, the primary meaning is commitment and loyalty.)

In that the man's response in Genesis 2:23 is a relationship formula addressed to Yahweh God rather than to the woman, it is as if the man were saying, "I hereby invite you, God, to hold me accountable to treat this woman as part of my own body."[8] (Cf. Eph 5:28–29; 1 Cor 7:2–7.)

As noted above, the language of "leaving and cleaving" also has covenant overtones because of its association with the God-people covenant relationship. "Leave" (*'azav*) is used extensively of people forsaking God (Jer 1:16; Hos 4:10). The Greek equivalent (LXX and New Testament) is *kataleipō*, with the meaning of leave behind. "Cleave" (*dabaq*) is used extensively for holding fast to God (Deut 10:20; Josh 23:8). The Greek equivalent here is *proskollaō* or *kollaō*, meaning to join closely.

Hosea is the first to label Israel's covenant infidelity as adultery, implying that marital infidelity is also unfaithfulness in covenant. The marriage analogy is prominent in the charges of covenant violation in Isaiah, Jeremiah, and Ezekiel.

Malachi 2:10–16 is the Old Testament *locus classicus* on marriage as a covenant. In a pattern of charge-question-explanation that runs through Malachi, this is the third of such disputations. In this block the specifics are: Yahweh no longer regards your offerings. Why not? Because you have been unfaithful to the wife of your youth. Scholarly opinions differ as to how to resolve the interpretative problems in this text. Although the Hebrew of this passage is difficult, a point of entry is the repeated words: faithless, one, covenant, profane, offering, wife of . . . youth.

Faithless, used five times, is variously rendered as deal treacherously, break faith, and forsake—toward one another and one's wife.

One is used four times. God (father/creator) is one, God's people are to be one family, and husband and wife are to be one (understanding v. 15 as in NIV: "Did not the LORD make them one?").

Covenant, used two times, is used for both "covenant of the ancestors" (God's covenant with the ancestors, their family covenant) and "your wife by covenant," setting these two covenant relationships alongside each other as interrelated. (The primary word for covenant in Hebrew is *brit*; in LXX it is *diathēkē*.)

Profane is used two times, with the meaning desecrate, unhallow. It describes the action toward the "covenant of the ancestors," and toward

---

8. Hugenberger, *Marriage*, 165.

the "sanctuary" (in the sense of making a mockery of worship, or perhaps referring to the people God loves).

Offering is used two times. Offerings were unacceptable because of unfaithfulness to covenants.

Wife of . . . youth, used two times, indicates the wives of many years who were being divorced in order to marry pagan women (daughters of a foreign god).

In Malachi 2:14, the covenant wife is called a "companion," *khaberet*, also translated as partner, and in the LXX as *koinōnos*, with the meaning of sharer or partner. Yahweh as "witness" (v. 14) indicates divine sanction in the marriage covenant. Several strong words punctuate the passage: abomination (Yahweh's assessment) and violence (what unfaithfulness and divorce do to those involved). Most translations of verse 16 have Yahweh saying, "I hate divorce." Yahweh could be the implied subject of the verb, but "hate" will need to be understood as it is used in Malachi 1:3, "I have hated Esau," and as Jesus meant it when he said, "Whoever . . . does not hate father, mother . . . cannot be my disciple" (Luke 14:26). The LXX of 2:16 offers another possibility (in my English translation), "But if you should hate your wife and put her away . . ." This fits well with the contextual situation in which pagan women were found to be more attractive. Hugenberger's paraphrase of 2:16 is: "If one hates and divorces {i.e., if one divorces merely on the ground of aversion} says Yahweh, God of Israel, he covers his garment with violence {i.e., such a man visibly defiles himself with violence} says Yahweh of hosts. Therefore, take heed to yourselves and do not be faithless (against your wife)."[9]

This is the first clear Old Testament reference to the spiritual "marriage" covenant informing human marriage also as covenant. Divorcing wives to marry non-Israelite women was a double covenant violation—compromising religious commitment by bringing in idolatry and breaking up marriages to do so. Yahweh had no regard for their worship because of their marital covenant breaking. Elizabeth Achtemeier opines that this is "a view which, if applied to modern society, would call into question the prayers and petitions of millions of American churchgoers." She contends: "This passage constitutes one of the most sublime understandings of the marital relation to be found in the Old Testament—an understanding

9. Ibid., 76.

consonant with the view of both Genesis 2:18–25 and the New Testament (cf. Mark 10:1–12; Eph 5:21–33)."[10]

Although not explicitly identified in the Old Testament as a required ratifying sign of covenant, sexual union is viewed as a "consummation" of marriage in a number of texts. Although Jacob thought he was sleeping with Rachel on their wedding night, he found himself in fact married to Leah based on sexual union (Gen 29:21–28). The fallout of pre-marital sex in Exodus 22:16–17 is that the man must make the girl his wife (not that she was in fact his wife because of their sexual activity, but he was required morally to take that step).

A common expression connoting sexual intimacy in the Old Testament is "knowing." "Now the man knew his wife Eve and she conceived" (Gen 4:1). When "know" is used relationally, it has to do with either covenant or sex. Hosea 2:19–20 is an example of where metaphorically "know," marriage, and covenant coalesce.

Marriage as covenant connotes a bondedness parallel with becoming "one flesh." As noted earlier, "one flesh" (*henosis*) is expressed by, but is much more than, sexual union. A married couple is "one flesh" not only while in the act of intercourse. Viewing marriage as a sealed commitment removes any notion of a "trial marriage." Walking away is not an option. Marriage does not come with a money-back guarantee if not fully satisfactory. Offense against the marriage by either partner draws the charges of infidelity (breaking faith), perfidy (deliberate transgression, treachery), and sin. To the extent that God is invoked and involved, the offense is sin against God. Gordon P. Hugenberger's extensive treatment of Malachi 2:10–16, *Marriage as a Covenant, Biblical Law and Ethics as Developed from Malachi*, is a defense of marriage as covenant. Hugenberger aggressively discredits all arguments against finding marriage as covenant in Malachi. In his polemical stance he fails, in my judgment, to take Jesus's reference to Genesis 1 and 2 as seriously as he should. The book makes a major contribution to a biblical understanding of marriage, but it stops short of spelling out the "so what?" of marriage as covenant.

In an effort to strengthen existing marriages and to raise the bar for those entering into marriage, the covenant marriage movement emphasizes marriage as covenant rather than simply a legal contract. This movement seeks to make it less easy to end a marriage through "no-fault

10. Achtemeier, *Nahum–Malachi*, 182.

divorce." Those choosing to put their marriages on this higher plane agree to receive premarital counseling including education on the meaning of marriage and to receive counsel if considering divorce. Generally it limits grounds for divorce to abuse, adultery, and felony with jail time. It may be entered into as a non-legal or a legal agreement. Louisiana was the first state of make covenant marriage available by law, and that in 1997. Other states have enacted similar legislation, and still other states are considering it. As might be expected, the movement is criticized as being too religious. It is being promoted as a non-compulsory option to counter the easy out notion, raising the standard along with a deeper understanding of what couples are getting into when they choose to marry. (Information on the covenant marriage movement is readily available on the Internet.)

In summary, the biblical view of marriage as covenant puts the marital relationship on a higher plane than convention, convenience, what's in it for me, or mutual benefits. It calls for commitment without reservations. It can and should be connected with faithful living in the covenant of grace God makes available in Christ.

C. LOVE

Hebrew (like English) has basically one word for love. That one word may be used all the way from God's love to professional "lovers." Greek, however, makes use of several words with more or less focused meaning, with agape love becoming dominant. In the transition from Hebrew to Greek, by way of the LXX, love in marriage takes on a heightened meaning.

The Hebrew word *ahab*, in its noun and verb forms, is used of the mutual love of Yahweh and his chosen people, of love between human beings (within and apart from marriage), of love of things (concretely, e.g., savory meat, and abstractly, e.g., law and wisdom), and of illicit love.

Perhaps this phenomenon of Hebrew vocabulary reflects a Hebrew view of things that makes less distinction between the sacred and the secular (spiritual and physical) than we commonly make because of the influence of the Greek tendency to dichotomize life. Contexts help to determine meanings but often leave open a danger of reading into the word what the reader wants it to say, such as with 2 Samuel 1:26.

The LXX predominately renders the noun *ahab* as *agapē*, and the corresponding verb forms similarly. The breadth of meaning of the Hebrew word for love can be seen in 1 Samuel 18, 20. Six additional Hebrew words (verbs and nouns) are used in a limited way in the Old Testament with meanings of longing for, setting love on, loving fervently, doting/lusting, parents loving children, mercy, beloved, and paramours.

Koine Greek, the language of the LXX and the New Testament, makes use of three words for love: *erōs*, erotic/sensual love; *philia*, family/friendship/nonsexual love; and *agapē*, volitional action on behalf of another. Classical Greek has a fourth word, *storgē*, which does not occur in either the LXX or the New Testament. Its meaning is similar to *philia*.

It is noteworthy that *agapē* is sparse in pre-biblical Greek, and that *erōs* is not found in the New Testament (and only twice in the LXX). The LXX translators' adoption of *agapē* as the dominant word for love has elevated the meaning of this term (and its verbal counterpart) to a new level. A key factor is that love is the fundamental foundation on which the concept of covenant is based—God's active love, which elicits reciprocal human love. Marriage as a covenantal relationship, which stands out in the Old Testament from Genesis 2 on, rests on this view of love that includes but transcends sensual and emotional feelings.

Gottfried Quell observed that "in Hebrew, so far as we can see, there is absolutely no possibility of expressing, even though it may be felt (2 Sam 1:26), the distinction between the two magnitudes of *erōs* and *agapē*. This means that the element common to both must have controlled the conceptions of the Old Testament authors so strongly that they did not feel any need for verbal variation. Hence we should find particularly instructive for a perception of this normative element in the content of the word those passages which indicate the spontaneous and irrational nature of love as a feeling that wells up from personality."[11]

How we understand what the common element is in the broad and sometimes seemingly dissimilar meanings of "love" may well provide a key piece in an understanding of God's design for human marriage. The LXX translators did not invent the word *agapē*, but they moved it to center stage and invested it with fresh meaning as the dominant word for love in the Greek Old Testament.

Therefore, the New Testament admonitions to husbands to love their wives do not exclude romantic and sensual aspects of their reciprocal love, but they do shift the fundamental motivation for marital love from getting to giving. I submit that this finding must receive due weight

11. Quell, "ἀγαπάω," 24.

in a biblical view of marriage. The difference between putting primary emphasis on giving rather than on getting is as profound as it is simple to understand and to apply.

Discovering that the goal of mature marital love, in the contours of agape love, majors in *giving* does not mean that there is not also a *getting* aspect of the love relationship. Beginners on the road of marriage may well be thinking and acting primarily on what they want to receive in the unfolding experience of life together. However, as a marital relationship grows, the partners should expand the horizons and find increasing fulfillment in a giving love. And this applies to the romantic and erotic aspects of their expressed love for each other.

This vision of investing more in giving than in getting in marriage is not a new perspective, of course. Marriage counselors know that spouses whose primary aim is what they can get out of the marriage jeopardize the health and future of their marriage. The point here is to underscore that love that majors in giving is integral to the biblical view of love and marriage. Human nature gets in the way of catching this vision, but those who know God's transforming love have the foundation for applying agape love to the full range of marital love. God's intent and provisions should raise the sights of Christians above the self-seeking pursuits of the prevailing culture.

Gerald W. and L. Marlene Kaufman share their learning from many years of marriage and family counseling in *Monday Marriage: Celebrating the Ordinary.* They see marriage partners expecting too much and giving too little to their marriage relationship. They urge couples to move from unrealistic expectations of getting to giving themselves in everyday covenant commitment. Jesus's saying, "It is more blessed to give than to receive" (Acts 20:35) is well known, but that principle has not been automatically applied to marriage and expressing love in marriage. It should be.

One aspect of sexuality in evidence in the biblical record is an emotional/psychological attraction and attachment between male and female prior to and within marriage. Given the holistic view of life and love in the Old Testament (and continuing in the New Testament), the big picture naturally includes examples of romantic love.

Amorous feelings show up in words and actions in the Old Testament. Examples range from seduction and obsession to highly sensuous love songs. The warnings against being seduced by sensual appeals

(Prov) and the sex sins in the several New Testament vice lists focus on misuse of sensual aspects of sexuality. They are not ruling out all sensuality. Sensuality is part of human sexuality, with morally proper and improper expression. The notion that the human body (with its hormonal chemistry and appetites) is inherently evil and must therefore be denied is not the biblical view. Sexuality is viewed as a good gift, with established boundaries of morality and propriety.

Abimelech figured out that Isaac and Rebekah were in fact husband and wife because he saw him fondling/caressing her (Gen 26:8), even though Isaac had said she was his "sister." Jacob loved Rachel, served seven years for her "and they seemed to him but a few days because of the love he had for her" (Gen 29:20). To avoid the snares of adultery, the advice in Proverbs 5:15–20 is: "Drink water from your own cistern . . . rejoice in the wife of your youth . . . May her breasts satisfy you at all times; may you be intoxicated always by her love." Although these lines may not show up as a Sunday-morning lectionary reading or in wedding meditations, they do reflect a straightforward view of sexuality within marriage.

Along with examples of right and wrong use of sexual feelings and urges, the Old Testament includes the Song of Solomon (a.k.a. Song of Songs and Canticles). Because of its erotic content, it was a Jewish saying (according to Origen and Jerome) that the Song should not be studied by anyone until he was thirty years of age. Incorporation into the Jewish canon may have been because it was attributed to Solomon and it was given an allegorical meaning. The marital status of the lovers is not entirely clear. Theories about the nature of the Song of Solomon fall into four approaches:

- Allegorical. Long-standing Jewish tradition sees it as an allegory of God's love for Israel. A Christian adaptation sees it as an allegory of Christ and the church (or the individual soul). Popular for seventeen centuries, this interpretation seems primarily motivated by discomfort with a literal reading. A variation is to view it as a typology, representing God and Israel, even though these lyrics never mention God.

- Cultic. This view proposes that it has roots in ancient cultic rituals in Jewish or pagan ceremonies, perhaps associated with weddings. Evidence of such a connection is scant, and a pagan background would likely have barred it from the Jewish canon.

- Dramatic. When the allegorical view fell into decline, efforts were made to assign characters, scenes, and plot, fitting the pieces into a narrative, perhaps about Solomon. This interpretation is forced on the text.

- Lyrical. The most obvious and least fanciful view is to accept it as a collection of love songs celebrating human love. In graphic poetic language, almost never read in public worship except for discretely selected lines, both male and female speak of physical attraction in romantic terms. "The Song of Solomon is a hymn in praise of sensual love with no minor strains of prudery or shame to mar its melody." [12]

The Song of Solomon reveals a mutually respectful attitude of the lovers for each other, whatever the assumed marital status, neither exploitive nor singularly self-gratifying. Several of the lesser used Hebrew words for love appear in the Song, along with eighteen occurrences of the primary Hebrew word, *ahab*. The LXX of the Song predominately uses *agapē* and never *erōs* in the many references to love.

Expressing the Yahweh-Israel relationship in marital terms, and the Old Testament frequently does that, assumes that the romantic overtones of the analogy were understandable. "The oft repeated prophetic comparison of the love of God for Israel with the love of husband for wife indicates that passionate love between spouses was so well known in ancient Israel that a reference to it in poetic simile could create the most powerful response the prophets wished to evoke in their audience." [13]

The New Testament contains little of a romantic/sensual nature, but it is not totally absent. The account of a woman wiping Jesus's feet with her hair and kissing them entails a highly sensuous act. In his response, Jesus neither is embarrassed nor does he scold her for expressing her love (Luke 7:38). Since the New Testament plays down the priority of procreation, what is said about marital relations implies a mutual desire for and enjoyment of intimacy, including sexual intimacy (e.g., 1 Cor 7:1–7, a text we will get to later).

Agape love is sometimes defined in such elevated terms that it supposedly is devoid of feelings. However, as noted earlier, the LXX redefined *agapē* to include the whole range of love. Therefore, in the New Testament

12. Cole, *Sex and Love*, 87.

13. Patai, *Sex and Family*, 48.

agape love should be understood holistically, with emphasis on the unselfish, giving nature of love in all relationships, including marriage.

The biblical story does not include the modern expression "falling in love" (and later perhaps "falling out of love"), although instances of infatuation do appear. With many marriages being arranged in Near Eastern cultures, premarital exploration of emotional chemistry did not have much opportunity. As noted above, there are examples of romantic attraction prior to and within marriage, but the basis for marriage was not primarily an emotional or glandular thing, as seems to be the case sometimes in recent times. Perhaps if we could quiz the Old Testament men who divorced their wives to marry others as to "reasons," they might approximate the phenomenon of falling in and out of love. (Deut 24:1–4 may imply that factor.) In neither the Old Testament nor New Testament is "falling out of love" an acceptable basis for divorce. Marriage involves the whole person, including feelings—romantic feelings. But agape love is primarily an act of the will.

The Bible recognizes in several ways that sexual attraction, as part of the human make-up, can and does readily shift to lust. In the Old Testament, the Hebrew verb *agab* and the corresponding noun have to do with lust, primarily referring to religious or spiritual prostitution of a people as a whole (rather than individual inordinate sexual desire). The prophets use strong imagery for the "whoring" after other nations, accusing God's people of behaving like "sluts" in their wanton unfaithfulness to him. Apparently they were well enough acquainted with lustful human behavior to understand the analogy. The Greek word *epithumia* sometimes has the general meaning of desire without moral specifications. It is the LXX rendering of the Hebrew word noted above and translated "covet" in the tenth commandment. In Proverbs 6:25, it has explicit reference to sexual attraction, and in Song of Solomon 5:16, as a summary of physical attraction of the "beloved," she says, "He is altogether desirable."

In the New Testament, we find *epithumia* in Jesus's teaching about looking at a woman with lust (Matt 5:28), and in Colossians 3:5, James 1:14–15 (as desire), and 1 John 2:16. A related word is *aselgeia*, with a meaning of sensuality or lewdness, sometimes translated as lasciviousness or concupiscence, words few people would be able to define, except in the general sense that they are not good. It is in several of the vice lists (Rom 13:13; 2 Cor 12:21; Gal 5:19; Eph 4:19; 1 Pet 4:3). Another term is "passion," *pathos*, several times coupled with *epithumia*, rendered as passionate desire/lust. First Corinthians 7:9 puts this human drive as a burning, using *puroō*, the verb for "burn." These human inclinations are only one aspect of the temptations encountered in faithful kingdom living. They come into the discussion here because they surface in texts having to do with marriage.

The arousal of desires of many kinds is a given. Here we are narrowing the focus to sexual desires. What does biblical revelation have to say about how we are to handle these desires? Unless we accept the rule that anything goes, we need both boundaries and self-control (or self-discipline). Regarding the boundaries, the Bible is clear that sexual activity is reserved for marital intimacy, with the understanding emerging in this study that marriage is for one female and one male. Although this boundary seems clear enough in general terms, the specific lines of what constitutes sexual activity, and particularly inappropriate sexual activity, requires careful discernment. Behaviors, both mental and physical, that generate erotic desire in either person are dangerous, if not over the line, even though short of genital stimulation or penetration. Many can testify regretfully to allowing themselves to get beyond the point of self-control. It's an old saw, but if you play with fire, you are likely to get burned.

As to self-control, the Old Testament references are almost exclusively in the wisdom books. The New Testament speaks of self-control in several ways, distinctively different from contemporary philosophical views. In Greek philosophy, self-control was viewed as a cardinal virtue, a do-it-yourself exercise in gaining mastery over all desires and thus being in complete control. The New Testament uses some of the same vocabulary, but with somewhat different meaning. The several forms of the word *enkrateia* are found in Galatians 5:23; 2 Peter 1:6; 1 Corinthians 9:25; and Titus 1:8. In 1 Corinthians 7:9, the application is specifically to control of sexual drives. The Greeks emphasized moderation and temperance, and some New Testament translations render this virtue as temperance. However, the Galatians 5 list has self-control as a fruit of the Spirit, not dependent solely on self-effort, but also not apart from human cooperation. For the Christian, disciplined living is integral with new life in Christ and the Spirit. A second word is used in the pastoral epistles, *sōphronismos*, translated as self-discipline, sound mind, and sobriety, without specific reference to sexual desires. In 2 Timothy 1:6, for example, the capacity to be "wise-minded" is a gift, needed to maintain a straight course in a seductive world. Word usage supports the sense that we need self-discipline, and that it is to be exercised as a spiritual gift. The adage, "You cannot keep the birds from flying over your head, but you can keep them from building nests in your hair," points out that we are not in full control of all the stimuli that generate desire, but we can and must control our responses.

Besides keeping sexual desires in their right place, responsible living entails paying attention to the effect of personal behaviors on others. The line between immorality and aesthetics may shift from time to time, but there is no room for Christians teasing the hormones of others under the guise of aesthetics (appreciation of the beauty of the human form). Provocative behavior is not part of the holy life.[14] Sexuality comes with a degree of inherent power, as the advertising industry knows and uses. Sexuality plays a part in attracting a mate. However, exploiting that power is a misuse of the gift of sexuality.

Word usage for sexual activity and intercourse indicates that love expressed in sex is normally a part of marital relations, and when the New Testament overlays the Old Testament, the usage supports the understanding that sex is proper only within marriage. Biblical Hebrew expresses human copulation primarily with two words. Genesis 4:1, as the first example, says "the man *knew* his wife Eve," a literal translation of *yada*, also used in the ordinary sense of knowing. In order to make the meaning clear for modern readers, dynamic equivalent versions render the expression as "had relations with," "had (sexual) intercourse with," and "made love to." The second is found in Genesis 19:14 and is an early example of the common literal translation, "lie with," for the Hebrew verb *shakab*, also used in the ordinary sense of lie down. Lot's daughters used their father to become pregnant. In Genesis 39:11–18, Potiphar's wife tried to induce Joseph to "lie with her," that is, have sex with her (probably not for the purpose of becoming pregnant). Some contemporary versions use "sleep with," with the obvious implication of engaging in sex. Most times it is a man lying with a woman, not a woman lying with a man, although these examples from Genesis have the women as more than passive partners.

The Greek equivalent of the Hebrew word *yada* is *ginōskō*. The LXX uses this word as one way to express sexual intercourse. It occurs also in this sense in Matthew 1:25, which notes that Joseph "knew" not Mary (had no marital relations with her) until she brought forth her firstborn son. The implication is that under normal circumstances, sexual activity

14. A speaker at a youth convention put the issue in perspective with this challenge, "Why are you advertising what is not for sale?"

goes with marriage. The LXX renders the parallel Hebrew word *shakab*, translated "lie with," as *koimaomai*, meaning sleep, when sexual intercourse is indicated. It is found in the LXX of Susanna 1:20, but not in the New Testament in this sense.

Sexual intercourse within marriage does surface in 1 Corinthians 7:3 in the language of mutual obligation, not limited to procreation. As will be noted in chapter 5, section B.6, "touch a woman" likely comes out of an ascetic view of human sexuality. Hebrews 13:4 calls for the marriage bed to be kept pure, not defiled by extra-marital sexual immorality.

Although singleness is the exception, especially in the Old Testament, the Bible does not openly promote marriage in the sense, "by all means get married." Rather, marriage is assumed to be the accepted practice. Similarly, the Bible does not promote sexual activity within marriage (other than "be fruitful and multiply") but assumes that it will take place. The moral codes do restrict sexual conduct to marriage. Laws (most explicitly in Leviticus and Deuteronomy) prohibit adultery, incest, rape, bestiality, homosexuality, and prostitution (sex for monetary gain). The fertility cults in the neighboring nations offered yet another opportunity for sexual activity. Israel did not stay free from these taboos. The Old Testament gives evidence of a double standard, not holding men to the high standard prescribed for women. Sacred prostitution continued despite the prophets. Yet when we add the New Testament teachings, the boundaries of sexual morality are clear. All that is left is sex within cross-gender marriage, with purposes including both procreation and pleasure. This fits with the overarching oneness (*henosis*) expressed as "one flesh," which is a good deal more than sexual intimacy, but does include sexual activity as an integral part of expressing giving love.

This is not to say that it is not really a marriage unless there is sexual activity. Health factors and temporary separation may make sexual expression impossible. Paul, in 1 Corinthtians 7, allowed for a hiatus for spiritual disciplines. However, sexual activity is normally a part of marriage and restricted to marriage.[15]

15. In the 1917 Code of Canon Law for the Roman Catholic Church marriage is primarily for the purposes of procreation and the education of children, and secondarily for mutual help and as a remedy for concupiscence. The 1983 Code designates no priorities and lists mutual help first. (Marthaler, *New Catholic Encyclopedia*, "Marriage Legislation," 206–7.)

For whether same-gender sexual activity, for purposes of pleasure and bonding, is also negated in biblical revelation, see the thorough, sensitive work of Swartley, in

Love, in common parlance, is so nondescript one wonders if it is a useful word. Yet, as the exploration has revealed, love is a key word in biblical revelation and teaching. Discovering the LXX use of *agapē* led to postulating that agape-love focuses more on giving than on getting. This attitude and action then applies to the full range of expressing love in marriage. This perspective goes against human nature and is learned by experiencing God's love in Jesus.

The reader can reflect on the interrelatedness of these weighty words: one flesh, mutual covenant, and giving-love. Together these constitute fundamental elements of God's design and provision for marriage.

Homosexuality. For a mutually respectful conversation on the pros and cons of recognizing same-gender commitments as marriage, see Grimsrud and Nation, *Reasoning Together.*

5

Intra-canonical Continuity and Movement

T HE BIBLE DOES NOT present a uniform picture of marriage. As noted earlier, the New Testament (both Jesus and Paul) grounds the teaching about marriage in Genesis 1 and 2—a notable evidence of continuity. The rest of the Old Testament (with vestiges showing up in the New Testament) reports some deviations from the intent as in the beginning. The patriarchs and the covenant people generally reflected the norms of their surrounding cultures, juxtaposed with calls to be different. Their request for a king and nationhood was based on their desire to be like the nations around them. The promises and attractions of the pagan religions (predominately fertility cults) led to compromises in moral standards for marriage. In response, God's prophets preached against their unfaithfulness.

Overall, strands of continuity are to be found within the canon. The examples of discontinuity serve to draw attention to the divine intent and provision of marriage. This section explores views and practices affecting marriage in which there is movement, both deviations and returns. First is a shift in a basic analogy.

A. ANALOGY OF HUMAN MARRIAGE AND GOD-PEOPLE

Whereas in much of the Old Testament human marriage is used to picture the mutual relationship of Yahweh and his people, in the New Testament (notably in Eph 5) the relationship of Christ and the church is set forth as the model for human marriage.

In the marriage metaphor in the Old Testament, human marriage (the known) illuminates the spiritual marriage of God and people (the unknown). As such, it may be seen as another anthropomorphism (e.g., God's arm, ears, eyes, etc.) accommodating expressions of spiritual reality to the limitations of human experience. The metaphor is used primarily to communicate what idolatry does to the relationship with the one true God, Yahweh. Prophets denounce covenant unfaithfulness in the sexual imagery of animals in heat and of whoring after other gods. Hosea's marital experience mirrors Israel's deviant behavior. The imagery includes promiscuity and prostitution as well as marriage per se.

The marriage metaphor, particularly as used in Hosea, leaves open the implication that since the "marriage" of God and his people is not between equals, human marriage is also to be understood to be between a greater and a lesser. We considered this implication in the exploration of covenant (in chapter 4, section B). To be sure, nothing of egalitarian mutuality can be based on this Old Testament metaphor. The comment has been made that male writers may have been quite comfortable with the analogy and these possible implications!

In Malachi 2:10–16, a text examined previously, having one father and creator calls for covenant faithfulness. Yet God's people have violated covenant (1) in going after other gods, and (2) in forsaking their marriage covenants. Here, in the last book the Old Testament, the nature of God and the exclusive covenant relationship of God and people become the basis for condemning marital unfaithfulness. Specifically they were divorcing their wives to marry foreign women, without realizing how that affected their covenant relationship with Yahweh.

Turning to the New Testament, Ephesians 5:21–33 is the unparalleled text proclaiming that the Christ-church relationship informs and shapes what the husband-wife relationship is to be. The marriage analogy is applied in reverse order from what we find in all but Malachi in the Old Testament. The why of this shift is not clear, unless anthropomorphic analogies are not needed on this side of Incarnation as they were before the Incarnation. The argument flows in the same direction in 1 Corinthians 6:16, where being one spirit with Christ rules out becoming one flesh with a prostitute. (Both of these New Testament passages have received more attention elsewhere: in the discussions of "one flesh" and "love" in chapter 4, sections A and C.)

In the Old Testament imagery, Yahweh is husband, "married" to his people. In the New Testament, Christ is the bridegroom and the church is the bride. In 2 Corinthians 11:2, Paul uses familiarity with espousal/ engagement as an analogy of establishing a relationship between believers and Christ, in anticipation of the messianic wedding banquet: "I promised you in marriage to one husband, to present you as a chaste virgin to Christ."

Both Testaments employ marriage as a central analogy. Since marriage is implicit in the Creator's design in the first chapters of Genesis and the last chapters of Revelation highlight the marriage supper of the Lamb, it requires us to probe deeply into what the Bible reveals of God's provision for marriage. The marriage analogy in the canon is a primary source for understanding God's intent for human marriage at any time.

B. EXAMPLES OF MOVEMENT

Evidence of some movement in recorded practices related to marriage is found within Old Testament and New Testament, and more significantly between the Old Testament and New Testament.

The observed differences have to do primarily with practices that relate to marriage, rather than with a fundamental shift in the revealed paradigm for marriage. Noting these shifts enhances the significance of the norms of the New Testament.

Here, as in some other parts of this treatise, the intent is to explore what is relevant to an understanding of marriage, not to go into an exhaustive study of the topics included. This is an area of biblical studies where differences between specific laws, the overall ethical/moral tone, and the reported practices need to be recognized and sorted out carefully.

1. Regarding Polygamy and Concubinage

Polygamy (literally meaning many marriages) in common usage refers to multiple marriages at the same time. It was practiced in Old Testament times as polygyny (married to more than one woman) rather than as polyandry (married to more than one husband), which was not permitted. The primary motivation for polygyny was the desire for children, sometimes because the first wife was barren. The same motive underlies the acquiring of concubines (wives, but of a lower rank) and the use of female servants of wives to produce children. A provision for levirate marriages (Deut 25:5, 7) may or may not assume the brother could be already married. Since the accounts report the multiple marriages of kings and other persons of wealth and position, it is not known how prevalent the practice was among people of ordinary means and status. However, polygyny served as a practical way to take care of an oversupply of women due to men being killed in battles and as expediency for childless couples. (In the comments that follow, polygamy will sometimes be used in the common generic sense, although polygyny would be more precise.)

The Torah permits one type of non-marital sexual relationship—concubinage. A concubine, *pilegesh*, is in sexual relationship with one man but without the legal privileges of marriage.[1] Political alliance also enters into the polygyny of kings, but that is the game of politics, hardly qualifying for calling it marriage.

In the prophet Nathan's rebuke of David for taking Uriah's wife for himself, he includes the words of Yahweh: "I gave you your master's house, and your master's wives into your bosom, and gave you the house of Israel and of Judah; and if that had been too little, I would have added as much more" (2 Sam 12:8). This reflects that it was considered lawful for the successor of a king to take over his predecessor's harem. There is no record that David married any of Saul's wives. In fact, only one wife of Saul is mentioned (1 Sam 14:50), and one concubine (2 Sam 34:7). Having received Israel and Judah, David could have chosen wives from among any of the virgins—the point being there was no reason to take another man's wife. Neither this passage nor any other in the Old Testament rules out polygamy. In anticipation of the Israelites wanting and having kings, Deuteronomy 17:17 has Moses warning against a king having many wives, who may turn his heart away. And that did happen.

Exodus 21:10–11 has a ruling that pertains to polygamy. The context has to do with the treatment of slaves, most likely those who sold themselves into slavery. Specifically it has to do with a man adding a second wife, with the first wife presumably being a slave. In such a case he is not to diminish for the first wife three basic rights that go with marriage—food, clothing, and something variously translated as marital/conjugal rights, love, or companionship.

In Hebrew the third term is *onah*, a word of uncertain etymology, found only here and in Hosea 10:10, where the meaning is also uncertain. The root is possibly the verb *un*, meaning dwell, though unattested as a verb in Hebrew. Coupled with food and clothing, the meaning here could logically be lodging/shelter. When we take into account the cultural shame of being childless, the meaning may well be that the first wife is

---

1. Gold, "Traditional Sources," 2.

not to be deprived of intercourse with the husband. The LXX has *homilia*, a word having to do with conversation and cohabitation. (Brenton has "companionship.") Verse 11 adds that if this husband fails to provide these three basic rights, she is free to leave, and he forfeits the price he paid for her. This added note is evidence that the ruling had to do with slave-wives. However, rabbinic tradition understood these marital rights as applying to all marriages and that neglect is a recognized basis for divorce, along with sexual unfaithfulness.[2]

The fact that Malachi (2:10–16) denounces divorce as well as marriage to foreign women implies that polygyny was not a live option at that time. If multiple wives were acceptable, then there would have been no reason to divorce "the wife of (their) youth," other than economics (which could have been a major factor). The biblical accounts show little evidence of polygamy in the post-exilic period. It is not clear why. Lack of reference to polygamy in the accounts does not necessarily mean it did not exist. Other than Deuteronomy 17:17, which says kings should not have many wives, polygamy is not addressed negatively in the Old Testament. Perhaps it was practiced less for practical reasons—because they no longer had kings, it was unaffordable, or the perceived need for descendants was greatly diminished. It might have been rejected on the theological grounds of being inconsistent with monotheism, but such is not the case. Somehow, having "wives" was acceptable, but having "gods" was not.

Both Jeremiah and Ezekiel employ marriage imagery in charging Israel (north and south) with covenant unfaithfulness. They have Yahweh "married" to both sisters. That could be construed as polygamy. Leviticus 18:18 prohibits marrying a sister of one's wife while the wife is living. As H. L. Ellison points out, when metaphor and simile are used in the relationship of Yahweh and his people, "They were no more than convenient approximations to the truth."[3] He goes on to note that behind any picture of a dual marriage is the reality that both kingdoms were only part of

---

2. Out of his extensive research into rabbinic writings, David Instone-Brewer writes: "Every Jew in Jesus' day knew about Exodus 21:10–11, which allowed divorce for neglect." He goes on: "Exodus says that everyone, even a slave wife, had three rights within marriage—the rights of food clothing, and love. If these were neglected, the wronged spouse had the right to seek freedom from that marriage" Instone-Brewer, "What God Has Joined," 28.

3. Ellison, *Ezekiel*, 94.

"all Israel." These instances of marriage imagery do not open the door to human polygamy.

Household gods show up at several points (Gen 31:25–35; Josh 24:14–23). The duplicity of syncretic polytheism in Israel was not eradicated until the time of the exile, although vigorously spoken against by the prophets. Even though polygamy is not explicitly condemned, the complicating effects of multiple marriages are readily discernable in the Old Testament narrative.

The specification in the pastoral epistles that an elder be "the husband of one wife" may be addressing the circumstance of polygamy being a part of a pre-Christian background. However, other options for understanding of this specification need to be considered.

The phrases "husband of one wife" (1 Tim 3:2, 12; Titus 1:6) and the converse, "wife of one husband" (1 Tim 5:9), get a variety of proposed explanations:

a. Marriage is a prerequisite for Christian ministries. However, the emphatic position of "one" in the phrase, and the fact that neither Paul nor Timothy are identified as married, practically eliminates this option.

b. Polygamous marriages exclude candidates from serving in leadership positions. However, to understand the phrase this way would require that "wife of one husband" implies polyandry, for which there is no evidence.

c. It prohibits second marriages, for whatever circumstances (death, divorce, desertion, as well as polygamy/concubinage). Remarriage after the death of a spouse is not categorically ruled out by Paul (1 Cor 7:39), and in fact is advised for younger women (1 Tim 5:14). Paul's preference for the unmarried status, based on eschatological and practical reasons, along with a refutation of false teachers who forbid marriage, hardly translates into a rigid prohibition of all second marriages, even if applied only to leaders. Remaining unmarried after the death of a spouse is commanded in some pagan and Jewish literature, although not expressed as "husband of one wife" or "wife of one husband."

d. A more-limited scope of prohibition against second marriage could be implied—that of remarriage after divorce. Explicit reference is made to marriage after death of a spouse (1 Cor 7:39), but not after divorce. (Also, 1 Cor 7:15 may be understood to allow remarriage after desertion has ended a marriage. See the discussion in chapter 6, section A.2.) Vocabulary is lacking for "remarriage" for any reason. This option needs to be read into the texts rather than it arising out of them.

e. The phrase means marital fidelity within marriage and also applies to sexual conduct after a marriage has ended. The Greek language and New Testament usage offer adequate ways to be specific about faithfulness within marriage and about sexual promiscuity when that is the intended meaning, but they are not used here. However, an emphasis on marital fidelity would not be out of line in the Greco-Roman culture. Since the same Greek word translates both as husband and man (similarly wife and woman), this possibility makes the phrases in question "a one-woman man" and "a one-man woman."

A constellation of texts suggests a linking of monotheism and monogamy (Mal 2:10, emphasis on one God; 2 Cor 11:2, espoused to one husband, Christ; Matt 19:6, Jesus emphasizing oneness; 1 Cor 6:16, one flesh, one spirit). These together with the repetition of "one husband, one wife" in the pastoral epistles may add up to the early church requiring those in public ministries to give witness in their marriages to the permanent union of Christ and the church. Thus the specification could have meant no second marriages for church leaders. Although this may be a plausible interpretation, we do not seem to have a definitive explanation.

A theological basis for monogamy is implied in the New Testament, if not explicitly argued. The New Testament neither reports nor entertains the possibility of polygamy. This does not mean there was no polygamy in the Jewish society of that time.[4]

Polygamy is defended by a few as consistent with the Bible, including the New Testament. One argument is based on 1 Corinthians 7:2, in which a different word occurs for "his own" (*heautou*) wife than for "her own" (*idou*) husband, although major translations make no distinc-

---

4. Jewish law did not rule out polygamy during the New Testament era. It was banned by Ashkenazic Jews in the tenth century AD. The Shephardic communities never outlawed it, and there is evidence of the practice in that branch of Judaism into the Middle Ages. Jews living in Islamic countries were more inclined to practice polygamy, since it was acceptable among Muslims (Schauss, "Marriage," 2).

tion. The contention is that the first "own" does not carry the exclusivity that the second "own" does, thus allowing polygyny but not polyandry. However, Acts 24:24 has "his own (*idia*) wife," and in Romans 8:3, speaking of God's own (*heautou*) Son, the Son is not viewed as one among others! The attempt to support polygamy from the Scriptures seems to be another example of finding what one wants to find.

As the gospel has moved into cultures where polygamy is practiced, the question comes up of what to do with families with more than one wife. The imposition of monogamous marital standards on Native Americans by European settlers resulted in women being pushed out to try to survive on their own. If a man's wives are to be reduced to one, what responsibility does he, and the community of faith, have for the welfare of those whose marriage has ended? Missionary practices have not been uniform regarding the Christian response to existing polygamy. Multiple factors come into play. Ezra's reforms did not seem to take into account what happened to ex-wives and children. The New Testament admonition regarding widows (1 Tim 5:3–10) is certainly not addressing an equivalent situation, but it's about as close as it gets to considering the fallout of imposed monogamy. That instruction gave primary responsibility to the extended family and then to the church. The faith community must be involved in the binding and loosing entailed in dealing with polygamous marriages/families and Christian faithfulness.

2. Regarding Prostitution

This practice needs to be included in a theology of marriage because it has to do with the sexual boundaries of married persons. The Old Testament accounts refer to two types of prostitution—cultic and common. Temple prostitutes are identified by both male and female forms of the Hebrew *qadesh*, with root meaning of consecrated (Deut 23:17–18).

Although strictly forbidden for Israel, cultic prostitution was prominent in the Canaanite religions, and was, in fact, incorporated into Israelite worship well into the period of the divided kingdoms (Hos 4:14; 2 Kgs 23:7). The primary objection to its practice is its association with pagan idolatry, perhaps more so than because of the sexual activity per se. In the several references to male cultic prostitutes, they may be assumed to have been for the benefit of female worshipers, although that is not specifically stated. Engaging in sex as honoring the deity in fertility cults in the Near East was common practice for both genders.

Common (secular) prostitution, generally using the Hebrew term *znut,* meaning fornication, has to do with granting sexual favors for a price. The practice emerges in the Old Testament at several points without explicit censure. Rahab is regularly identified as a harlot. The incident in Genesis 38 involving Judah and his daughter-in-law, Tamar, implies that prostitutes were part of the cultural scene, and that visiting a prostitute was not considered irregular for a man. Judah was unmarried at the time, his wife having died. His sin had more to do with his failure to keep his promise to Tamar.

In the Middle East, from biblical to Muslim times, males were having sexual relations outside of marriage, even though it was not openly condoned. Females were guarded closely, in part because of paternity concerns. However, prostitution was openly practiced, with evidence of it into the latter days of the monarchy (1 Kgs 22:38; Prov 9:14–15, Jer 5:7). The laws prescribed that priests were not to marry prostitutes (Lev 21:14) and that the gain from prostitution (by both female and male temple prostitutes) was not to be brought as an offering to the Lord (Deut 23:17–18). Proverbs warns against the seductive ways of professional prostitutes. Proverbs 7 depicts a married woman (whose husband is not at home) offering herself sexually. Most translations identify her as an adulteress (v. 5), rather than a prostitute, because of her unfaithfulness in marriage. Prostitution is never looked on favorably in the Old Testament.

The metaphor of prostitution (whoredom) for religious apostasy is prominent from the time of the deviation at Baal Peor (Num 25) through the prophets (notably, Jeremiah, Ezekiel, and Hosea). In the graphic language of "whoring after the nations," the sisters, Israel and Judah, compromised their covenant "marriage" with Yahweh. In Ezekiel 16:30–34, they are accused of even going beyond whoring for hire to paying their lovers in their solicitous behavior. The Israelites must have had enough acquaintance with prostitution (in Israelite as well as pagan culture) to understand the metaphorical use by the prophets.

In marked difference from the Old Testament, the New Testament leaves no room for prostitution (cultic or secular) or any sexual activity outside of marriage. The term *porneia,* which the LXX uses for both Hebrew words noted above, is sometimes translated as fornication (which has the narrow definition of sex involving singles), but clearly it also applies to all sexual immorality. The view of sexuality is no longer that it is acceptable for men to get sexual satisfaction wherever they can get it. The New Testament view of the sexual drive is that it not only can be but must be controlled. It does not sanction the argument that since a person has a sexual appetite, it deserves to be satisfied. Sex within marriage (with the uniform assumption of a male-female covenant) is affirmed as God's creative intention. For singles the rule is abstinence apart from marriage.

Paul's response to the libertine views on sexual activity in 1 Corinthians 6:12–20 goes beyond the general moral boundary of "flee fornication." For a believer to be joined to a prostitute, he says, is a violation of union with Christ (as noted in chapter 4, section A).

Paul also specifically addresses God's will for Christians regarding sexuality in 1 Thessalonians 4:3–8, in sharp contrast with the practices of the Greco-Roman world. That will is holiness, which means avoiding sexual immorality. Interpreters and translators do not all agree on how to understand verse 4, with two key words having several possible meanings. Jacob W. Elias analyzes the options and builds a convincing case for the meaning "that each one of you know how to control your own body," rather than it being about how to get a wife.[5] The necessity and possibility of control is clear, as over unleashed sexual passion and lust (in the experience of those married or single).

Paul recognizes the strength of sex drives in his "concession" to marriage (1 Cor 7:6). Yet the wonder of marriage could hardly receive stronger affirmation than in the analogy in Ephesians 5:21–33. Hebrews 13:4 also gives marriage a stamp of approval. (More on singleness in chapter 5, section B.5.)

3. Regarding Definitions of Adultery

The Hebrew word *naaf*, translated adultery, means sexual intercourse in violation of the marriage covenant. In the Old Testament, for a married man that meant sex with the wife of another man (including an engaged girl), and for a married woman it meant sex with men other than her husband. This double standard required unconditional fidelity only of the women. For example, David's adultery involving Bathsheba was technically not against his wives but against Bathsheba's husband. This agrees

---

5. Elias, *1 & 2 Thessalonians*, 139–41, 149–51. Elias has an extensive discussion of the teaching of this text.

with wives being considered in some sense property of husbands. The surrounding cultures held similar views about adultery. In the Roman/ Greek world, the cardinal rule about consorting with another man's wife was to avoid getting caught while invading another man's domain.

The Decalogue forbids adultery (Exod 20:14; Deut 5:18), and Leviticus prescribes the punishment as death (Lev 20:10; cf. Deut 22:22–29), usually by stoning. The penalties vary according to gender and marital status. Although in some cases both are to be put to death, the laws are harder on women than on men. Concern for purity of blood lines contributes to the seriousness of the sin of adultery. A man must be sure about the paternity of the children in his household.

The prophets use the language and imagery of adultery to decry Israel's covenant unfaithfulness by going after the idolatries of surrounding cultures (Hos 2, 4; Jer 3, 5, 7, 23, 29; Ezek 16, 23). Hosea says Israel owes exclusive loyalty to Yahweh as a wife does to her husband. The same words are used (Hebrew and LXX) for marital infidelity and for Israel's spiritual adultery.

The teaching of Proverbs, notable in the poems of 2:16–19; 5:1–6, 7–14, 15–23; 6:20–29, 30–35; and 7:1–23, is the most explicit of any in the Old Testament about marital faithfulness. Likely it stems from a breakdown of marriage covenant fidelity at the time of writing. The teaching is addressed particularly to young men, calling them to be faithful to their own marriage and not go after other women, married or unmarried. Adultery of any kind is wrong because it is hurtful to the wife by violating the basic marriage covenant with her.[6]

Not until the New Testament does the definition of adultery sweep aside the old double standard practices evidenced in some of the Old Testament. In the New Testament, all marital infidelity, whether by male or female, is adulterous. Jesus (Matt 5:27–28) included lustful desire as well as intercourse. The lopsided moral rules of the day stood exposed as Jesus confronted the accusers in John 7:53—8:11, not by condoning adultery but by insisting on even definitions. Jesus's words in Mark 10:11, "Whoever divorces his wife and marries another commits adultery against her," specifically broaden the definition of adultery. Here it is adultery

---

6. Several essays in John W. Miller's commentary on Proverbs elucidate the contribution of Proverbs to what the Bible says about marriage. See "Text in Biblical Context," 86–89.

against his wife rather than the Old Testament position that it was against the husband of the other woman.

The Greek word family *moicheuō, moicheia,* with the meaning illicit intercourse, is also applied to unfaithfulness to God (Matt 12:39; 16:4; Mark 8:38; Jas 4:4). Strictly defined, adultery has to do with marriage infidelity, and fornication, *porneia,* has to do with sexual activity between the unmarried. However, that distinction is not maintained in the LXX or the New Testament. Both terms are employed to designate Israel's unfaithfulness to Yahweh. Jesus's teaching on divorce includes the factor of adultery. (The section on divorce, in chapter 6, section A.2, has more on the effect of adultery on marriage.)

4. Regarding Fruitfulness/Posterity

The original assignment to male and female humans included "be fruitful and multiply." It was reaffirmed to Noah (Gen 9:1, 7). The promises to Abram included innumerable descendants. Terms used include seed, offspring, posterity, and children. Concerns about barrenness and posterity gave rise to polygamy, use of maid-servants, and the provision of levirate marriages. Having a wife who is a "fruitful vine" (Ps 128:3) and fathering many children were considered marks of divine blessing. Having a future depended on having biological descendants. The worst imaginable end was to be childless. "Record this man as childless," is Yahweh's end-of-the-line judgment on Coniah (Jer 22:30). The Babylonians killed all of the sons of Zedekiah in his sight and then put out his eyes (Jer 52:10–11).

Notably absent in the New Testament is the imperative of fertility that characterizes much of the Old Testament. "Marriage ceases to be a means of ensuring a survival beyond death."[7] Procreation is not explicitly mentioned in connection with sex. By implication, the purposes for women, marriage, and sex are moving beyond the making of babies. The relative silence of the New Testament on posterity and name perpetuation does not mean that these values were no longer shaping life. The New Testament writers and teachers may have simply assumed the cultural norms. Yet the new covenant perspectives point to a changing view regarding fruitfulness and posterity. When Elizabeth and Zechariah had their promised baby, the relatives and neighbors wanted him named after his father, but both mother and father said his name would be John. Paul's

---

7. Von Allmen, *Companion to the Bible,* 256.

advice to Timothy (1 Tim 5:14) regarding younger widows is that they marry, have children, and manage their households. Childbearing is assumed to be normative in that setting.

Another aspect of this shift is that the spiritual family takes precedence over the biological family (Matt 12:46–50; Rom 9:8). The New Testament affirms marriage as good and holds children in high regard, but the driving priorities have changed in the kingdom of Christ. Furthermore, the future rests on faith in the resurrection rather than on biological posterity. These factors significantly alter the New Testament theology of marriage. (Attitudes toward singleness are closely related, and we turn to that next.)

5. Regarding Attitudes toward Singleness

The Creator's assessment that it was not good for "the man" to be alone and the charge to multiply translated in Old Testament times into a near-universal practice of marriage, with producing children as top obligation. Not to marry and produce children was viewed as shameful for a woman and a dereliction of responsibility for a man. For Jeremiah to remain single at Yahweh's mandate made the unmarried prophet stand out in his culture as a sign of impending doom. Prostitutes and women past child-bearing age were about the only singles.

One explanation of why little is found in the Old Testament regulating the sexual activity of unmarried males and females is that very few who were sexually mature were unmarried. Girls were married at twelve and thirteen, boys at fourteen to eighteen. Unbetrothed females were virtually inaccessible. The absence of sexual rules is not to be taken as evidence of indifference to sexual behavior.

The New Testament maintains that marriage is normal and honorable, but also recognizes singleness as a valid option. Jesus was single (*The Da Vinci Code au contraire*) and had numerous single persons among his followers. These included both male and female associates, for example, Mary, Martha, Lazarus, Mary Magdalene, Jesus's mother (after Joseph's death), and apparently most of the Twelve. Alongside Christ and the church being a model for marriage, the relationship of Jesus with single persons provides a model for human singleness that has received too little attention. This would seem to be on a different track from the notion of spiritual "marriage" with Jesus, as taught by Roman Catholicism.

Hebrews 13:4 unequivocally affirms marriage as honorable and underscores God's rule of sexual fidelity. The provocation for this admonition may have been the ascetics who taught against marriage and sex within marriage, or from those at the opposite pole who bought into the cultural looseness that did not respect the exclusivity of marriage. Although the noun "marriage" usually refers to a wedding, here it does seem to mean an ongoing marital relationship. The first two clauses of Hebrews 13:4 do not have any verb in them. Most translations have supplied an imperative, "Let marriage be held in honor ... or let the marriage bed ..." but several opt for an indicative, "Marriage is honorable ..." The phrase "in/by/among all" can be taken either as masculine (held in honor by all, married or unmarried) or as neuter (highly esteemed in all respects). This text includes both fornicators (*pornous,* those with sexual irregularities, whether married or not), and adulterers (*moichous,* those unfaithful to the marriage vow), thus covering the full range of sexual immorality.

Remaining unmarried is viewed positively, under certain conditions, but is not held to be a superior status. While Paul recommended being unmarried for practical and eschatological reasons, he recognized that celibacy is not the gift of all, and he stringently opposed an asceticism that forbade marriage (and that forbade sex within marriage, as noted above). Both the married and the unmarried make up the New Testament cast of personages.

Paul's counsel to both unmarried women and unmarried men in 1 Corinthians 7 reflects the New Testament view of fruitfulness and posterity (discussed in the previous section). The reason for allowing and affirming singles to marry is to accommodate sexual drives and not specifically so they may have children (cf. 1 Tim 5:14, noted above). This is a significant shift from Old Testament views of singleness.

6. Regarding Views of Women

Much of the marriage relationship hinges on attitudes toward women. It therefore becomes necessary to trace the way women are viewed throughout the canon. Texts come into focus that have been misinterpreted, as well as texts that have not been given due recognition.

The Old Testament has mixed signals. On the one hand we find language connoting complementarity, companionship, and partnership, and examples of women respected as capable leaders. On the other hand, male dominance is evident in women belonging to men in a unilateral sense (daughters under their fathers' protection and control, and wives under their husbands'). The language of "giving in marriage" reflects that view of women. One motivation for keeping unmarried daughters as virgins was that they were worth more as virgins when negotiating marriages. The cultures of the Near East made and still make even more of this point than is explicit in the Old Testament.

Inequities in the laws gave more rights to men than women (e.g., in matters of rape, divorce, and inheritance). Although the daughters of Zelophehad were granted their father's inheritance because he had no sons (Num 27:1–11), the daughters were required to marry within the clan to keep the property within the family of the father (Num 36:6–12). Differences in the time of uncleanness after giving birth to a son or a daughter reflect the relative values of male and female (Lev 12:1–5).

Although not the only recognized function of women, bearing children certainly came to be ranked as top priority. The culture considered barrenness a shame, leading to polygamy, childless wives offering their female servant to their husbands, and the levirate provision for childless widows. Lot's daughters carried out their incestuous scheme, as one of them put it: "to preserve offspring through our father." The perspective found in Song of Solomon was highlighted in the section on romantic love in chapter 4, section C.

Jesus and the New Testament writers project a somewhat different view of women compared with the Old Testament. We do find evidence of a male-dominated culture at times. For example, in the feeding of the five thousand in the Synoptics, Matthew has the count as "five thousand men, besides women and children"; Mark as "five thousand men"; and Luke as "about five thousand men." However, as we will see, there is movement toward a higher regard for women. The picture the New Testament presents stands in striking contrast to the prevailing chauvinistic Greek and Roman valuation of women. Greek views are illustrated by the comment, "We have harlots for our pleasure, concubines (pallakas) for daily physical use, wives to bring up legitimate children and to be faithful stewards in household matters."[8] The Old Testament view of women as of secondary importance regresses rather than advances in Judaism. Jewish views of male superiority are evident in the strong preference for male children

---

8. Ps.–Demosthenes, quoted by Oepke, "γυνή," 778.

over female children.[9] A much different view is reflected in these sentences from the Talmud: "Honor your wife, for thereby you enrich yourself. A man should be ever careful about the honor due to his wife, because no blessing is experienced in his house except on her account."[10] It is not to be thought that Judaism was totally repressive with regard to women and wives. As has been noted, the Old Testament vocabulary does include expressions of respect and tenderness.

New Testament perspectives particularly relevant to marriage include:

1. Luke's attention to women (some single, some married) being among Jesus's followers, thus going against the custom of the day.

2. The mention, by name, of a number of women in influential roles and ministries in the early church. Among them are several married couples. What is said of Priscilla is noteworthy. In two of the three references to Priscilla in Acts 18, she is mentioned before her husband, Aquila, which leaves the distinct impression that she was directly, perhaps primarily, involved in "explaining the way of God more fully" to Apollos and in other aspects of ministry.

3. The explicit equality set forth in 1 Corinthians 7:1–7 with respect to husband and wife. It must be remembered that the teachings in 1 Corinthians that have to do with marriage were not written as a comprehensive treatise on marriage. They are Paul's response to specific questions and tensions arising in the church in the pagan culture of Corinth at that time. Therefore, we need to go slowly in generalizing from specifically dated issues. Texts in chapters 6, 7, 11, and 14 call for careful attention, while keeping in mind their contextual setting.

In chapter 7, Paul is responding to matters raised in a letter to him. The saying, "It is well for a man not to touch a woman," is probably best taken as a quote from the letter and put in quotation marks, as many translations do. His answer is of the nature of, "Yes, but . . ." In some respects he agrees with the statement, but for quite different reasons from those to whom he is responding. In chapter 6, he vigorously rejects the notion that sexual looseness does not matter. In chapter 7, he answers the

9. Ibid., 781.
10. Cohen, *Everyman's Talmud*, 165.

ascetic position that married people (although they stay married) should eliminate sex ("touch a woman" means sexual intercourse). So, while Paul himself prefers the celibate life, and recommends it for those so gifted, he also affirms non-celibate married life. (More on other parts of 1 Cor 7 later.) With this background in mind, we can appreciate better the contribution of 7:2–7 to a theology of marriage.

The remarkably balanced wording is outstanding. This striking feature must be given due weight alongside what Paul says in verses 2a and 6 that these positive comments about marriage are by way of concession rather than command. Paul's unmistakable preference for remaining unmarried should not obscure or override the revolutionary thrust of the implicit mutuality in this text. (NRSV wording of vv. 2b–5a follows the Greek text closely. The arrangement is added.)

each man should have his own wife	*and*	each woman her own husband
the husband should give to his wife her conjugal rights	*and* *likewise*	the wife to her husband
for the wife does not have authority over her own body, but the husband does	*likewise*	the husband does not have authority over his own body, but the wife does
do not deprive	*one another*	except perhaps by agreement . . .

The reference to "authority," *exousia*, in verse 4, specifically that in marriage both husband and wife lose authority over their own bodies, is especially noteworthy in that issues of authority are prominent in 1 Corinthians. Although focused here on bodies (the physical aspect of marriage), the relinquishing of autonomy in marriage is not limited to sex. Paul touches on a fundamental understanding of marriage, in sync with the inclusive phrase "becoming one flesh" (*henosis*). Paul's bold statement stands in conflict with the admonition of independence in Sirach/ Ecclesiasticus 33:19: "To son or wife, to brother or friend, do not give power [*exousia* in LXX] over yourself, as long as you live."

First Timothy 2:11–15 is a text in which some find a basis for male superiority. Most translations have the instruction to be about a woman and a man, although several translations, in footnotes, allow that it may be about wife and husband. As noted earlier, the Greek words can have either meaning. Here the issue at hand seems broader than marriage. This text comes into the discussion here because of the wording "have authority over," specifically about a woman not being permitted to have authority over a man. The word for authority is not the same as in 1 Corinthians 7:2–6 *(exousiazō)*. Here the key word is *authentein* (the infinitive form of *authenteō)*, occurring only here in the New Testament. It carries the sense: to domineer, to order, to control. The words translated "silence/keep silent" connote quietness, without causing disturbance. She is to learn, in full submission (the same word family as in Eph 5:21), but not teach. Paul's ruling here seems to be localized, because he does not give similar instructions to churches in other locations. In fact, he affirms the ministries of women such as Priscilla and Phoebe and expects older women to teach what is good and to urge younger women to love their husbands and children (Titus 2:3–5). This text in 1 Timothy has been understood to allow women to teach other women and children, just not teach men. However, the sentence structure does not support appending "a man" to teaching in the way it does to exercising authority over.

The key to trying to understand the apostle's agenda in this text is in verses 13 and 14. Is he grounding his ruling in Genesis 2 and 3, or does he bring in the creation and deception factors regarding Eve for another reason? Readers today are not likely to be aware of the views about women in the province of Asia in the first century. Richard Clark Kroeger and Elizabeth Clark Kroeger document the prevailing views in pagan religions.[11] For example, in Anatolia the Great Mother was viewed as the source of all life; Artemis was the mother goddess, the goddess of birth; Cybele was worshiped as the Mountain Mother. The notion of female primacy went so far as to say the Mother produces life without male assistance. Gnostic teaching elaborated these strands with emphasis on knowledge of feminine origins as source of salvation. These views go far beyond Genesis 3:20: "The man named his wife Eve, because she was the mother of all living." Paul, writing to Timothy in Ephesus, sets the record straight from Genesis 2 and 3. He counters the identification of the pagan goddesses with Eve and the elevation of the female to prime position. First, Eve was not first in order of creation, and second, what she was first at was to be deceived and to deceive. That observation from Genesis is not to be taken as proof of male supremacy, as has been done.

11. Kroeger, *I Suffer Not,* 105–12.

John the Baptist came before Jesus, but that does not make him greater. The comment that the serpent knew to tempt Eve because he knew the man would not yield is reading into the account what one wants to find. Verse 15 makes reference to salvation and childbearing. Being saved as a result of bringing children into the world does not accord with the New Testament understanding of salvation by receiving the gift of grace. The preposition "through" (*dia*, here followed by an accusative) can just as well mean "through the experience of," thus standing over against the negative theme of Genesis 3:16 (BDAG). A common interpretation of this verse is to take childbearing as Child-bearing, the Messiah being born of a woman.

The Kroegers propose an alternative translation of verse 12. They understand "to teach" as the content of the teaching rather than the act of teaching, explained in the words following as proclaiming to be the author of man. The Gnostic notion was that Eve was the creator of Adam. They offer the optional flow of thought as: "I do not permit woman to teach nor to represent herself as originator of man but she is to be in conformity [with the Scriptures] [or that she keeps it a secret]. For Adam was created first, then Eve."[12] They have found the LXX and early Christian writings to understand *authentēs* (the noun form of the infinitive in v. 11) as author/originator/creator. The questions surrounding the key word commonly translated as "have authority over" and awareness of the Gnostic/pagan elevation of Eve and the female provide plausible options for understanding Paul's agenda in this problematic text. The last part of verse 15 returns to the themes of verses 9–10, switching the focus from Eve (she) to women (they). Since these verses do not bear directly on marriage, we can leave this pericope with some questions not fully resolved.

We find elements of mutuality in marriage in some Old Testament accounts and more implicitly in several New Testament texts. The term "equal-regard marriage" is being used by some contemporary writers as a label for the Christian tradition regarding marriage. Don Browning defines "equal-regard marriage" this way: "Equal-regard marriage is based on a Christian principle that makes it possible for the husband and wife to have equal access to, equal privileges in, and equal responsibilities for participation in the public world, the wage economy, politics, and domestic obligations. It doesn't mean wife and husband have to be identical in their

12. Ibid., 103.

roles. It means that they in principle are free to work out their roles in an equal way depending on their natural inclinations, their talents, their various concerns, their various pursuits. They may not be identical but they can negotiate that equality."[13]

A much-misused text is Galatians 3:28: "No longer male and female, for all of you are one in Christ Jesus." Paul does not here erase all differences between male and female (or between Jew and Greek, or slave and free). The point of the text is unity in Christ, with equality of worth, but not obliteration of sexual differences.[14] This is to say, equal regard and mutuality do not add up to unisex.

Because 1 Corinthians 11:3–16 is sometimes used in hierarchical societies (both in marriage and in general) to support male dominance, and because it also contains the word and concept of authority, this text deserves attention here. Most English renderings are more interpretations than translations. It is a rare "translation" that is free of interpretation. So, we tend to choose translations that support what we want them to say![15]

Traditional translations have tended to lead us to think we know what the text says before we read it carefully. When we examine this text and translations more closely, we notice that a number of translators understand verse 3 to be about husbands and wives, while others take the reference throughout verses 3–15 to be to men and women in general. As noted above, the Greek words can be translated either as man or husband, woman or wife. In verse 8 the reference is to man and woman, rather than to husband and wife. The terms may not have the same meaning throughout this pericope, but unfortunately the English translations do not let us know that a judgment has been made as to the meaning in a given verse. Either way, the marriage relationship enters the picture, and so does the translator's view of marriage.

The structure of the Greek text of verse 3 is not as neat as a formal chain of command would have us assume. If Paul had in mind an over-under, hierarchical sequence of God—Christ—man (husband)—woman (wife), he did not express it in a straightforward fashion. The three lines are not grammatically parallel. The order of the words and the use and

---

13. Browning, "Putting Marriage," 6–7.

14. See Yoder, *Politics*, 177.

15. See Swartley, *Slavery*, 164–77, for an analysis of divergent interpretative differences with regard to this text and other Pauline texts having to do with women.

non-use of an article with nouns is not uniform. A literal translation (retaining word order and articles) is:

a. *pantos andros hē kephalē ho Christos estin,*

   of every man the head (the) Christ is,

b. *kephalē de gynaikos ho anēr,*

   head and of (a?) woman/wife the (or her) man/husband,

c. *kephalē de tou Christou ho theos.*

   head and of (the) Christ (the) God.

Articles with Christ and God are common in Greek and do not require a definite article in translation. The article with head, in line a, may be indicating the subject (when the subject and object are both nominative with a copulative verb). If so, that makes head the subject of the clause. The English translations are divided on this matter, with most having head as the subject. Since lines b and c have no stated verb, the same copulative verb, *is,* is to be implied in these lines, but "head" does not have an article in lines b and c, as in line a. These differences illustrate the non-symmetrical construction in these lines. These grammatical uncertainties then give rise to translators and commentators taking some liberties.

The Greek word translated "head," *kephalē,* can have several divergent meanings, and it does have in biblical usage. In 11:3–13, "head" does not have the same meaning in all of the nine occurrences. In some instances it refers to the top part of the human anatomy. However, in verse 3 it has a relational meaning. In subsequent verses the meaning of "head" will need to be determined by careful attention to the context.

To discern Paul's intended meaning here, we might look for help in the way the word head is used elsewhere, first in 1 Corinthians. The only other occurrence is in 12:21, where head refers to a body part without any sense of priority over other body parts. When we turn to other Pauline usage, we find the word in plural in Romans 12:20, with head signifying the person. The only other occurrences are in Ephesians and Colossians, included here, although whether they are in the Pauline corpus is questioned.

Ephesians 1:22 says: "He [God] has put all things under his [Christ's] feet and has made him the head over all things for [or *to,* or *through*] the church, which is his body . . ."[16] The clear overtones of headship here are those of status, first place position.

"We must grow up in every way into him who is the head, into Christ . . ." (Eph 4:15). Here "head" connotes that Christ is both the goal and source of growth in the whole body, the church.

"For the husband is the head of the wife just as Christ is the head of the church, the body of which he is the Savior" (Eph 5:23). The head metaphor here is relational, comparing the husband-wife relationship with the Christ-church relationship. This text has close similarities with 1 Corinthians 11:3. The context in Ephesians particularly draws attention to how Christ exercises his headship in a service of love.

"He (Christ) is the head of the body, the church" (Col 1:18). In this context head points to source and priority.

"For in him (Christ) the whole fullness of deity dwells bodily, and you have come to fullness in him, who is the head of every ruler and authority" (Col 2:9–10). Christ is the source of fullness and the one who is supreme over all.

Colossians 2:19 describes those who seek to disqualify those in Christ as "not holding fast to the head, from whom the whole body, nourished and held together by its ligaments and sinews, grows with a growth that is from God." Christ, as head, is the source of life, nourishment, and growth for the body.[17]

Back to 1 Corinthians 11, in verse 3 a picture of status is not to be ruled out categorically, with an over-under relationship. However, we need to recognize that the relationship is not the same in each case. One way to designate the difference would be to use "Head" in lines a and c and "head" in line b. God as head of Christ raises the issue of subordinationism within the trinity (some texts have Jesus emphasizing the priority of the Father and others affirm that he is one with the Father). The sequence in verse 3 could be viewed as headship implying source, although not exactly the same in each case. Verse 8 notes that woman was out of the man, but then verse 12 goes on to observe that man is born of woman. Verse 11 affirms that "in the Lord" man and woman are not independent

16. See Neufeld, *Ephesians*, 78–79 for discussion of the options for the dative form of *ekklēsia*.

17. For more on the Old Testament and New Testament meanings of "head" (and headship) see my essay, "Head and Body," 293–94; Schlier, "κεφαλή," 673–81; Blankenhorn, *Does Christianity Teach?*

of each other, strongly implying that "in the Lord" the playing field is level, although in the natural order of fallen human nature dominance tends to prevail.

The precise meaning of "head" in verses 4 and 5 is especially complex, since references to physical head and relational head seem to be mixed together. According to verse 4, a man is not to pray or prophesy with his head covered, contrary to Jewish law and practice. The *tallith* was and is worn by Jewish men out of reverence for God and as acknowledgment of guilt and condemnation for sin. But for those who are in Christ Jesus there is now no condemnation. So for a Christian man to wear the *tallith*, Paul says, is to dishonor his head (in this case "Head," from verse 3, that is, Christ who has removed his condemnation).

The question inevitably arose, what about women, especially in the Christian assembly? Jewish oral law specified that for a woman to appear in public with her head uncovered had the connotation of her being an adulteress, and she could be divorced because she had dishonored her husband (her relational head). It was Jewish custom that a woman accused of adultery was to have her head shorn or shaven. The Jewish law provision seems to be implied in verse 6. Although a woman (as well as a man) in Christ Jesus is no longer under condemnation, and thus need not continue to wear a token of guilt, Paul concedes that if being uncovered is going to result in disgrace and shame (assumed to be likely), then "let her be covered/veiled" (as the present passive imperative is rightly rendered). Understood this way, Paul is permitting her to be covered/veiled, but not commanding it.

Interpretative differences show up in several places. In verse 7 some commentators make a crucial point out of the wording that a man "is the image and glory of God, but the woman is the glory of man." Genesis 1 makes no mention of anyone being the "glory" of God. Further, both male and female (humankind, LXX, *anthrōpos*) are made in the "image" of God. (Unless one takes Gen 1 to refer to an androgynous being—challenged and dismissed above—"image" applies equally to man/husband and woman/wife.) Any male priority distinction must be based on Genesis 2, but as noted above, Jesus combined Genesis 1 and 2 and treats them as a unit. Here in 1 Corinthians 11, to the extent that Paul makes anything out of the woman being made out of and for the man, he balances it with the reality that now a man owes his existence to a woman.

If one is looking for a way to support male supremacy, verse 7 could be cited, but the meaning of "glory" here suggests several other lines of thought. In a sense humankind is the climax of God's creative work, crowned with glory and honor (Ps 8:5). And if we allow for any separation of the man and the woman in creation, the woman is the ultimate step. Paul takes pride in the Thessalonian believers, writing, "You are our glory and joy" (1 Thess 2:20). A husband may well think of his wife in those terms.

Verse 10 is a defining text for observing interpretative and translation differences. A literal rendering of the Greek text is:

> *dia touto opheilei hē gynē exousian echein epi tēs kephalēs dia tous angelous*

> on account of this ought the woman authority to have on/over the (her) head on account of the angels.

Authority has to do with ability and right. The preposition *epi* often has the meaning "on." Here it is connected to authority and followed by a genitive, as it is in Revelation 2:26 and 14:18 where the meaning clearly is "over." Taking Paul to say that a woman ought to have authority over her head (i.e., her own head) is a straightforward rendering. Several of the more obviously imposed interpretations on translations are these:

> KJV: "For this cause ought the woman to have power on her head because of the angels." Then in the margin, regarding "power": "that is, a covering in sign that she is under the power of her husband."

> NAB: "For this reason a woman should have a sign of authority on her head, because of the angels."

> NASB: "Therefore the woman ought to have a *symbol of* authority on her head, because of the angels" ("*symbol of*" in italics in NASB to indicate added words).

How authority (*exousia*) became a symbol/sign is a long story.[18] Nobody would say that "the Son of Man has a sign of authority to forgive sins." Yet most major translations have either "sign (or symbol) of authority" in 1 Corinthians 11.

Thus while some see this passage as clearly supporting male dominance, including the marriage relationship, others understand that Paul's

---

18. Bushnell, *God's Word*, pars. 251–70.

purpose was to stop the practice of men veiling in worship (the *tallith*). As regards women, this view sees Paul as permitting women to veil, but not requiring it (and ideally they have no need of a veil). This construes verse 13 and 14 not as questions but declarative statements. The word order of a sentence, in Greek, is the same whether it is a question or a simple statement, and there is no interrogative word in these sentences. Only the punctuation, which has been added along the way of transmission, distinguishes a question from a declarative sentence.

The wording and grammar allow the Bushnell rendering of verses 13 and 14 to be feasible: "It is proper for a woman to pray unto God unveiled. Nor is there anything in the nature of hair itself that teaches you that if a man wear it long it is a dishonour to him, while if a woman have long hair it is glory to her, for her hair has been given her instead of a veil."[19] Matters of modesty and respect for societal conventions still apply. The several interpretative views are not only broad range but also highly contradictory.

The primary reason for bringing 1 Corinthians 11:3–16 into this study is not to offer a definitive interpretation of this text but to illustrate how preconceived views affect translations and commentaries. English translations continue to be used to support diverse views of Paul's teaching in this pericope. The details of the grammatical construction in Greek deserve careful attention. They open up plausible interpretations that challenge traditional views. This means that deductions from many English translations of this text cannot serve as fixed points by which to interpret other texts.

Although spousal abuse goes both ways, notions of male authority have contributed to some husbands with Christian identity abusing their wives in all sorts of ways (physically, verbally, sexually, and emotionally). Even suggesting that domineering, abusive behavior is justified by Scripture is to take Old Testament intimations of women as property beyond/below what the Old Testament says. Using a text like 1 Timothy 3:4, which says a bishop "must manage his own household well," to justify keeping a wife "in her place" by whatever means ignores the Old Testament, to say nothing of the respect accorded to women in the New

19. Ibid., par. 247.

Testament. Some wives who are being abused have been led to believe it is part of being "submissive."[20] Several additional observations follow.

The expression "marry and are given in marriage" is used by Jesus about marriage in this world (Matt 22:30 and parallel accounts). Saying that men marry and women are given in marriage parallels Old Testament concepts and reflects the way first-century Jews would think and speak of marriage. However, Paul in 1 Corinthians 7:9, 28, 36, 39, and 1 Timothy 5:11, 14 has the verb "marry" applying equally to women, moving away from the idea of a transfer of ownership from father to husband.

A phrase in 1 Corinthians 14:34 suffers common misuse: "women should be silent . . . should be subordinate, as the law also says." Reference Bibles and commentaries often cite Genesis 3:16 as where the law says anything like that. But is that what God's words to Eve mean? Do they not predict/describe what will be the effect of sin rather than prescribe what is supposed to be? In Genesis 3 only the phrase "he shall rule over you" is interpreted by some to be God's law. At issue is English usage of shall/will and the translator's choice of words that leave an implied connotation. The effects in the natural world have been acceptably countered (e.g., herbicides, air-conditioned tractor cabs). The relational effects of sin should certainly be addressed by the realm of redemption even more than difficulties in producing food. That Genesis 3:15 is descriptive is evident in the biblical story of humanity.[21]

A second factor must be respected in understanding this phrase in context. The sharp tone of Paul's words in 14:36–38 imply reaction to something. If we take verses 34–35 as what Judaizers were saying, the flow makes much more sense. (This text should be added to those in which translations identify with quotation marks words from others to which Paul is responding, e.g., 1 Cor 6:12–13; 7:1) Verse 39 naturally follows verse 33, interrupted by the exchange of the verses between. The "law" then becomes Jewish oral tradition, not a reference to Genesis 3 or any

20. The *Confession of Faith* (1995), Article 22, includes "abuse of children and women, violence between men and women" among the forms of violence that are not the will of God, along with war, racial hostility, abortion, and capital punishment.

21. Bushnell, *God's Word to Women*, pars. 105–6. Bushnell traces how the translations of Genesis 3:16 have devolved through the centuries. She contends that male bias has affected the wording, resulting in faulty interpretation and application of the text. She notes how the teaching of the Babylonian Talmud, in the "ten curses of Eve," has further distorted views on the Genesis account. The interpretation here of 1 Corinthians 14:33–40 reflects Bushnell's analysis.

Old Testament text. The arrangement of 1 Corinthians 14:33–40 that follows respects the tonal changes. (NASB wording; arrangement, font appearance, and quotation marks by EDM.)

> For God is not a God of confusion but of peace, as in all the churches of the saints.
>
> *"The women are to keep silent in the churches; for they are not permitted to speak, but are to subject themselves, just as the law also says. If they desire to learn anything, let them ask their own husbands at home; for it is improper for a woman to speak in church."*
>
> **Was it from you that the word of God first went forth? Or has it come to you only? If anyone thinks he is a prophet or spiritual, let him recognize that the things which I write to you are the Lord's commandment. But if anyone does not recognize this, he is not recognized.**
>
> Therefore, my brethren, desire earnestly to prophesy, and do not forbid to speak in tongues. But all things must be done properly and in an orderly manner.

The admonition to husbands in the version of the Household Codes in 1 Peter 2:13—3:7 includes wording that is sometimes misused. The sentence, 3:7, does present translation problems. Since Greek has no way to distinguish between wives and women, and since the word usually translated husbands is also a common word for men, the admonition could be broader than married men. However, since the primary verb is literally "dwell together," a marital relationship is implied. "Knowledge" in this context is not implying the husband is to be the brains in their married life, but that husbands should keep important factors in mind and remember the difference that Christ makes in marital and community relationships.

The phrase identifying a woman as a weaker vessel (frequently translated as weaker sex) begs for explanation. Weaker in what sense? Sheer physical strength, perhaps. But in terms of longevity, fortitude, and spiritual vitality, either we need to say Peter was wrong or that he meant something else. Perhaps the point is to remind the men that they have advantages women do not have. In that culture particularly, women were less powerful than men, and therefore deserved intentional consideration by Christian husbands. Regarding the admonition for Christian husbands to show consideration to their wives, Erland Waltner comments: "In the larger context of the continuing call to deference and reverence, it includes a call to respect the full personhood of the woman in a marriage relationship."[22] This text thus meshes with the admonition in Ephesians 5 to give due respect to and to sanctify the spouse. Peter backs this call with two reminders. Wives/women are joint-heirs with husbands/men in the grace of life. That implies equal status. Furthermore, failure to show deference and honor is a hindrance to prayer. Peter connects the attitude of a husband toward his wife to the fundamental spiritual discipline of prayer. Strong words, indeed, and the application goes far beyond avoiding what may be regarded as abuse.[23]

With regard to the views of women in the biblical data, we have observed Old Testament practices and regulations that limit the relative importance of women in relation to men. We have also observed attitudes and activities reflecting a high regard for women as also being in the image of the Creator. In the New Testament we have found vestiges of the traditional male superiority mentality, plus a number of significant practices and teachings that affirm equality between women and men, without erasing sexual differences. The Bible does have examples of sexism but not support for attitudes and practices that do not hold women and men in equal regard.

All of these examples of intra-canonical movement have bearing on understanding God's provision and intent for marriage. The deviations serve to heighten appreciation for God's design for marriage in the human family.

---

22. Waltner, *1 Peter*, 99.

23. Achtemeier, *1 Peter*, 218. "The point is clear: men who transfer cultural notions about the superiority of men over women in the Christian community lose their ability to communicate with God."

Helpful discussions of the New Testament view of women will also be found in Stagg, *Woman in the World*, and Swartley, *Slavery*.

6

What About . . .

MARRIAGE, AS OBSERVED IN the biblical records, has its twists and turns. Some of them are positive and some negative. Undoubtedly there were many fine marriages in Old Testament and New Testament times, but not all were without challenges. In this section, several opportunities and several potential problems are taken into account. We will look at the problems first.

A. PROBLEMS ENCOUNTERED

1. Abuse

Abuse within the marriage relationship is not explicitly reported in the biblical accounts. Abuse within marriage does take place and may well have in ancient times. Abusive behavior does damage to the marital relationship. But the Bible does not define what kind or degree of abuse puts a marriage back at square one. That the violence of physical and emotional spouse abuse is sinful behavior seems clear. Whether the abuser is male or female, silent endurance on the part of the victim is not a biblical mandate, any more than biblical teaching justifies physical or verbal abuse. As with a violation of faithfulness in marriage, violation of personhood strikes at the core of the covenant relationship. Whether abuse is reason for divorce will be discussed in the following section.

Distance and separation can provide needed safety. Children in the home may complicate the helpful options. Likely both partners in an abusive relationship need help, but they may not admit it. The faith community can and should become involved. A church family is a family system, and when part of the family is stressed, the whole family is affected. Rather than trying to define the degree and intensity of abuse that destroys a marriage and allows for formal acknowledgment in divorce (which the Bible does not do), resources for the healing of persons and relationships need to be sought and provided.

Domestic violence of whatever sort, of spouse, children, and the elderly, is primarily a control issue. The "need" to control stems from a personhood deficiency, often insecurity. In the marital relationship, abusive behaviors indicate a lack of the essential mutual respect that must be at the heart of marriage. "Home Shouldn't Be a Place that Hurts" is a Mennonite Central Committee brochure available in English and Spanish designed to encourage an end to silence on domestic violence. (Abuse comes up again under divorce, which follows.)

2. Divorce and Remarriage

God intends marriage to be a lifelong commitment and relationship. Divorce, disallowed in certain circumstances and acknowledged (but not commanded) in others, constitutes a serious violation of covenant in God's sight. Jesus set the record straight with some Pharisees that Moses did not command divorce but regulated it as an accommodation to hardness of heart. "From the beginning" God had not left the back door open on marriage. The Deuteronomic regulations presuppose the practice of divorce but do not treat men and women equally. With several exceptions, husbands could get "male-order" divorces, and according to added Jewish rules, could do so for almost any trumped up "reason."

Deuteronomy 24:1–4, to which the Pharisees referred in their question to Jesus (Matt 19:7; Mark 10:4), has suffered misuse then and now. It is made up of a series of hypothetical conditions in verses 1–3 ("suppose . . ." NRSV), followed by a conclusion with reasons in verse 4. Verses 1–3 constitute the protasis (the "if" factors). The Hebrew uses *ki* (two times) with Qal imperf. LXX uses *ean* with aorist subj., implying that these several actions could happen. None of the elements are in the form of command. In simplified wording, EDM, the protasis is:

a. if a man takes a wife, but is displeased with her, and gives her a letter of divorcement

b. she becomes another man's wife, and if he dislikes her, and gives her a letter of divorcement

c. or if her second husband dies

Verse 4 is the apodosis (the "then" factor), the law governing the given situation. The Hebrew uses a Qal imperf. with the negative *lo*. LXX uses a fut. mid. indic. with the negative *ou*. Both languages connote that he is not to take her back, because that is an abomination. Although the regulation no doubt reflects marital anomalies of the time, its intent is not to authorize divorce, to specify grounds for divorce, or to establish proper procedures for divorce. Its primary purpose is to flatly prohibit return to the previously divorced partner after contracting a second marriage (called palingamy)

Although this text rightly understood is restricted to remarriage to a first husband after a divorce and marriage/divorce to a second husband, the rabbis later debated the meaning of *erwat dabar* ("something objectionable," NRSV) in Deuteronomy 24:1 as defining a reason for divorce. The LXX has *aschēmon pragma*, ("something unbecoming," Brenton). The imprecision of these words gave Hillelite rabbis room to include "any cause" as reason for lawful divorce. The variety in translations reflects the imprecision of the Hebrew and the interpretative leanings of the translators—some uncleanness, some unseemly thing, something indecent, something objectionable, something unbecoming.[1] This restriction, though not prohibiting the practice of divorce, would have served to restrain frivolous divorce. The Hillel school took this non-proscription of divorce as supporting their lax view of divorce "for every cause." The Shammai school held to stricter rules for divorce. (In Deut 24 adultery is not a factor, since adultery was punishable by death. More on the reference to Deut 24 by the Pharisees below.)

The primary point of these four verses does speak to the not uncommon situation in which remarriage follows divorce, by at least one partner. (The Deut 24 ruling does not include the possibility of a wife divorcing her husband, but the New Testament does.) Before one of them remarries, the possibility of reconciliation and reunion is open, but after either is remarried that option is closed.

Several Hebrew words with meanings of put away/send away/dismiss receive the translation divorce. One word, *kritut,* from the verb to cut (as to cut a covenant) with the sense of sever/cut off, is used in the formal bill of divorcement (Deut 24:2–3). In Malachi 2:14–16, divorce, *shalakh,* as a verb, is described in Hebrew as dealing treacherously with a wife, and in

---

1. See Hugenberger, *Marriage,* 76, for a grammatical analysis of this complex paragraph.

LXX as abandoning/forsaking. Most translations have Yahweh saying in Malachi 2:16, "I hate divorce." (This text was explored in chapter 4, section B, with an alternate interpretation.) The Old Testament has only a few examples of marital separation, perhaps because of the expected custom of returning a dowry, which was too expensive. According to evidence from the Talmud, divorce came to replace stoning in cases of adultery.

Two Old Testament accounts pose something of a moral dilemma for us: Hosea 1–3 and Ezra 9–10. Hosea 2 presents a divorce court scene, with the dual cases of Hosea versus Gomer and Yahweh versus Israel. The statements, "She is not my wife," and "I am not her husband," rescind the marriage vows. The elements of courtship and betrothal later in the chapter confirm that the marriage had ended. But how can a God who is so strongly opposed to divorce instruct Hosea to divorce his unfaithful wife and say he is reluctantly divorcing Israel? Divorce imagery also describes Yahweh's attitude and action in Jeremiah 3:6–13. In human ways of thinking about this dilemma, Yahweh took the lesser of two problematic options and directed Hosea to do the same. Somewhat similarly, Yahweh temporarily jeopardized his reputation among the nations when he disciplined his people with exile to Babylon.

Adultery, in both cases, did deadly damage to the marriages. Divorce acknowledges that the "marriage" is broken, which Israel did not acknowledge in her duplicitous behavior. Remarriage to the same "wife" meant starting over, within God's patience, love, and grace.

Ezra confronted the spiritual effects of intermarriages with foreign women. His solution to the problem was to command the men of Judah and Benjamin to put away (divorce) those wives. And over one hundred men (priests, Levites, and laymen) did send them away with their children. The disruption of families is hard to imagine. Even such drastic reform measures did not end the intermarrying, according to Nehemiah 13:23–31. (More about intermarriage and Ezra's call for divorcing foreign wives in the next section on mixed marriages.)

When we come to the New Testament we find Jesus's teaching regarding divorce in Matthew 5:31–32, 19:3–9 (with a parallel account in Mark 10:2–12), and Luke 16:18. In the section of the Sermon on the Mount characterized by "you have heard that it was said . . . but I say unto you," Jesus moves from redefining adultery (Matt 5:27–30) to the issue of divorce. The progression is deliberate. "One could paraphrase: 'While I'm on the topic of adultery, what about the man who puts away his wife with the excuse of a divorce bill?' In this passage Jesus is not as concerned about a man divorcing an unfaithful spouse as he is with the irresponsible divorce because of the selfishness of the male. He challenges the previously undisputed power of the husband's patriarchal right."[2]

The precipitating question in Matthew 19:3–9 and Mark 10:1–12 is a question about divorce. In both of these accounts, the questioners have ulterior motives, but the context of the question is not clear. In Matthew the question is about the lawfulness of divorce for any cause. The specification "for any cause" may reflect the ongoing debate between the followers of Hillel and the followers of Shammai. Hillel's school promoted "any cause" divorce, which allowed divorce for any frivolous reason, whereas the Shammai school held that only immorality was just cause for divorce. In the Markan version of this exchange, the question is simply, "Is it lawful for a man to divorce his wife?" Stated that way, the Pharisees, knowing Jesus's opposition to divorce, may have tried to put Jesus in conflict with the Scriptures, which they understood to permit divorce. Notice that the verbs "command" and "allow" in Mark are reversed from the way they occur in Matthew. In Matthew the Pharisees seem to understand that Moses (Deut 24:1–4) *commanded* the letter of divorcement, which Jesus puts as Moses *allowing* for divorce, because of the hardness of people's hearts. In Mark, where Jesus asks, "What did Moses command you?" Jesus may likely be referring to Genesis 1 and 2 rather than Deuteronomy 24.[3]

However we choose to understand the questions and motives, Jesus quickly shifts the focus from divorce to marriage, as he refers to Genesis 1:27 and 2:24. Jesus is thereby saying that discussion of divorce and remarriage must be put within the framework of God's intention for marriage. The original plans did not include provision or regulations for divorce.

Jesus's further words about divorce, remarriage, and adultery (in both Matthew and Mark) do occasion much debate. Commenting on Mark 10:1–12, Timothy Geddert says that how we interpret Jesus's teaching depends on what question we understand that Jesus is answering. Geddert notes two possibilities:

---

2. Ewald, *Jesus*, 58.

3. On the relationship of Matthew and Mark on this exchange between Jesus and the Pharisees, see Ewald, *Jesus*, 47–49, and Gardner, *Matthew*, 289–90.

1. When is divorce and/or remarriage wrong?

2. Is it still adultery if I first divorce my present wife and then marry the person I want to sleep with?

As to answers, "If Jesus is answering the first question, his answer here is 'Always.'" But this approach creates tension not only with the message of the rest of Scripture, but also with the focus of Mark 10:1–12, where Jesus is not preoccupied with rules about divorce.

"If Jesus is answering the second question, his answer here is 'Yes.' Jesus is then insisting that God calls for marital faithfulness; he does not permit legal games to justify sin. This approach is better because it preserves the focus of the preceding section, and because it leaves unanswered the question whether in different circumstances divorce and/or remarriage can ever be right."[4]

The "exception clause" (Matt 5:32; 19:9) has been challenged because it is not included in Jesus's similar teaching, Luke 16:18. However, the textual evidence is strong that it is genuine. It is best understood as a statement of the obvious. Marital unfaithfulness strikes at the very heart of marriage. Apparently Luke did not deem it necessary to go beyond the general rule. One example of general rules having exceptions is the common dictum three strikes and you're out. But if the catcher drops the ball, the batter may run for first. The exception clause cannot be dismissed by saying, "We are not sure what the exception clause means, so we will go with Luke's rule, which is perfectly clear."

This exception clause "also makes clear Jesus' chief point for the divorcing couple: *If the wife is not guilty, then the husband is.*"[5] Jesus is particularly addressing divorce "for any cause" (for other than sexual unfaithfulness, "frivolous"). Since remarriage is assumed to take place after divorce, the second marriage adulterates the first one (unless already adulterated by unfaithfulness). In both Matthew 5 and 19, the exception is for *porneia*, which covers every kind of illicit sexual intercourse (not to be limited to premarital sex). These statements by Jesus (Matt 5 and 19) assume that remarriage will follow divorce. It is clearly not ruled out or prohibited. Remarriage following divorce was anticipated also in the ancient laws.[6]

4. Geddert, *Mark*, 230–31, 240–41.

5. Ewald, *Jesus*, 60.

6. Ibid., 122.

Jesus statement, "Therefore what God has joined together, let no one separate," is sometimes quoted as proof that it is impossible to separate what God joins (for life), and thus (from that point of view) a second marriage after divorce is a continuing state of adultery. However, prohibitions by their very nature are not against the impossible, but against what ought not to be done. A present imperative of *chōrizō* (separate) with the negative *mē* means Jesus's injunction is, "Stop doing what you are doing." Jesus makes a strong statement that must be respected. But the text does not support the position that in God's sight only death can end a marriage. Jesus did not say, "You can't," but "Don't." Although admittedly an argument from silence, Jesus, in John 4, did not tell the woman at the well that she was in fact still married to her first husband in God's sight (supposing him to be living).

The other major passage that speaks of divorce is 1 Corinthians 7. In this part of the letter Paul responds to questions posed in a letter to him. The questions having to do with divorce and remarriage include: (a) Should married persons divorce out of kingdom concerns? (b) Should a person who has become a believer divorce an unbelieving spouse? (c) If an unbelieving spouse separates, is the believer free to remarry? (d) Is a widow/widower free to remarry?

Paul's answers are: (a) If married, stay that way. But if they do separate for expressed spiritual reasons, they should remain single or be reconciled (vv. 10–11; 17). (b) In mixed marriages, the believer should not divorce an unbelieving spouse, if the partner is willing to remain in the marriage. Such a marriage is a "Christian" marriage (vv. 12–14). (c) If the unbelieving spouse leaves, the believer is "not bound" (v.15a). It may be inferred from this that desertion is ground for divorce. Verses 15b–16 refer back to verses 12–14. The verb for "separate" in verse 15 is *chōrizō*, the same verb as in the prohibition of Jesus in Matthew 19:6 and Mark 10:9. As to "not bound," a perfect passive of the verb, *douloō*, meaning under bondage or enslavement, with the negative strongly implies that desertion breaks the marriage bond and the remaining partner is free (to remarry). Some hold that this freedom does not include remarriage, but here Paul does not make that limitation specific as he does in verse 11. "We therefore infer that in such cases he is not promoting remarriage nor forbidding it."[7] (d) Death does break the marriage bond, and the remaining spouse is free to

---

7. Ibid., 88.

marry, only in the Lord (meaning, another believer), verses 39–40. The Greek word here is *deō*, a synonym of the one in verse 15, also a perfect passive, meaning bound or tied to. The same verb occurs in verse 27, where the meaning is "married." [8]

The question still remains, is abuse a basis for divorce? Paul's understanding in 1 Corinthians 7:10–11 is that abandonment or desertion by an unbelieving spouse dissolves that marriage. Passive neglect leaves the believing partner free to remarry, after divorce. But what about the active neglect of physical, verbal, or emotional abuse?

The Hillel school could put spouse abuse under "any cause" going back to Deuteronomy 24:1, as well as under the extreme neglect of not providing the basic requirements based on Exodus 21:10, written into marriage contracts. The Shammai school limited just cause to adultery. Speaking out of a culture in which the husband has the dominant position in marriage, some rabbis have condoned wife-beating as chastisement and education. Through the centuries Jewish rabbis have been slow to approve abuse as a basis for divorce. Jewish women have typically been slow to leave an abusive relationship because of fear of losing their children. [9]

Abuse does havoc to marriage, as do adultery and desertion. It violates the respect of personhood that enables *henosis*. Although not specifically addressed in the Bible, it is parallel with the designated factors that decimate marriage. It follows that divorce is one way to acknowledge the deadly damage. The extent and nature of the abuse that make it fatal in a given marriage need to be assessed. As with other factors, divorce is not mandatory, but if the relationship is to continue, it will require essentially starting over.

For Christians to resort to divorce from each other involves the audacity to tell Jesus that not even he can heal a stressed marriage. "Divorce among believers is a denial of the central message and experience of the reconciling gospel." [10] Although consideration of what divorce is saying to Jesus should give Christian couples pause, the reality may be that some couples should never have gotten married in the first place. Maybe Jesus should not be expected to fix all bad choices. As a probate judge has put

---

8. Romans 7:1–4 is not really about divorce but about being free from the law by being dead in Christ. (The law, Deut 24:1–4, does not hold a remarried divorcee guilty of adultery.)

9. Graetz, "Domestic Violence," 1.

10. Lederach, *Spiritual Family*, 19.

it, "Our problem is not that it is too easy to get a divorce, it's that it is too easy to get married." The covenant marriage movement would seem to be a step in the right direction.

3. Mixed Marriages

Both testaments recognize marriage between unbelievers. In the Old Testament exogamy (marriage outside the ethnic family) was strongly discouraged, in favor of endogamy (marrying within the clan) in Deuteronomy 7:1–6 and 1 Kings 11:1–8, 16:31–32. A primary reason was the danger of pagan influence being brought into Israel. This was a realistic concern, as the example of Solomon (and many others) shows. A secondary concern was to keep the bloodlines clean. In Malachi's time (2:10–16), men were not only marrying foreign wives but also divorcing their Hebrew wives in order to do so. (Noted in the discussion of covenant in chapter 3, section C.2.) Ezra's call to put away (divorce) foreign (pagan) wives, to which the guilty husbands complied, sending them away with their children, was a drastic measure to try to rid the returned exiles of pagan influence. The issue was religious purity, not ethnic purity. Ezra was not calling for ethnic cleansing. Nehemiah demanded a promise to quit intermarriage with foreign women. The historical relationship between Ezra, Nehemiah, and Malachi depends on which of the disputed dates for Ezra is accepted. Regardless of the timing, all three acknowledge intermarrying was having a detrimental effect on the religion of the covenant people.

Alongside the endogamy examples of Isaac and Jacob, we find notable examples of exogamy (Joseph, Moses, Rahab, and Ruth). The practice of intermarriage with foreigners is not unusual in the Old Testament. What would be labeled inter-racial marriage is also part of the picture (Num 12). For the most part, the Old Testament accounts reflect a justified concern about the pagan influences coming into Israel through marrying outside the faith community. Why did they not see intermarriage as an opportunity to expand the community of faith? It appears that usually the pattern was to accommodate to the religions of foreign wives rather than to win them to serving Yahweh. That may reflect the shallowness of the convictions about their being people of the covenant. Even though Ezra's extreme measures were motivated by spiritual rather than ethnic concerns, within the Old Testament canon the books of Ruth and Jonah stand in tension with Ezra's solution in his day.

The New Testament addresses mixed marriages in a number of texts. The stipulation in 1 Corinthians 7:39 that widows may marry again, only in the Lord, likely reflects the general rule in the early church. Although 2 Corinthians 6:14–16 does not mention marriage in the teaching, "Do not be mismatched with unbelievers," marriage would certainly be a pertinent application of the rule. In the New Testament, believers are to enter into marriage only within the spiritual family.

The term "mixed marriage" includes more than believer and unbeliever. Roman Catholicism has held that marriage between a Roman Catholic and a Protestant is a mixed marriage. Since 1908, in the *Ne Temere* decree, marriages performed by a Protestant minister are now considered valid, but with church-imposed restrictions and provisions for annulment (thus avoiding the step of divorce).[11] Small includes the saying, "For a child of God to marry a child of the Devil is to have Satan for his father-in-law!" and adds, "What a complication of the in-law problem that is!"[12] Paul does not say if the discipline of "shunning" (1 Cor 5:9–13) is to be exercised within a marriage relationship. How far shunning extends into marital relations has been debated, with mixed outcomes.[13]

Paul addresses the specific issue of one spouse (either husband or wife) becoming a believer in 1 Corinthians 7:12–24. His word, from the Lord, is that if the unbelieving spouse is willing to stay in the marriage, the believer is not to initiate divorce to get out of a mixed marriage. Rather, by staying the believer has opportunity to be a holy influence in the household (sanctifying the unbeliever and the children). Further, the continuing Christian presence may lead to the unbeliever being saved. In the realistic event that one spouse in an existing marriage becomes a believer, resulting in a mixed marriage, the believing spouse is admonished to stay in the marriage with a "mission" stance and behavior.[14]

---

11. Boettner, *Roman Catholicism*, 351.

12. Small, *Design for Marriage*, 23.

13. See Neff, "Ban," 219–22, for Anabaptist understandings and practices regarding the ban.

14. Verse 16 in RSV is rendered as questions, implying negative answers, as if to say: Do you think you really can change your spouse? This is a minority interpretation. NRSV renders it, "Wife, for all you know, you might save your husband. Husband, for all you know you might save your wife." See also Ewald, *Jesus*, for helpful exposition of 1 Corinthians 7 on mixed marriages.

The several Household Codes do not assume that in the paired relationships both are Christians. The admonition to slaves recognizes the possibility of mistreatment by unbelieving masters (1 Pet 2:18–25), and sets the possibility of unjust suffering alongside the unjust suffering of Christ. The transition phrase in addressing wives (1 Pet 3:1), "in the same way," has been used to tell mistreated wives that their only option is to accept without complaint whatever cruelty they experience from their husbands. But slavery and marriage are not parallel, and using the advice to slaves to tell abused spouses to tolerate abuse is unwarranted. If the abusive spouse is a professing Christian (as is sometimes the case) options of confrontation (Matt 18:16–20) offer alternatives to silent endurance. Peter offers two-fold advice. On the negative side, retaliation is not the Christlike way. On the positive side, Peter offers a way to use Christian freedom to challenge society's norms.

In the Greco-Roman world, wives were expected to adopt and comply with the religion of their husbands. However, Peter does not tell Christian wives to worship the gods of their unbelieving husbands. Nor does he tell them to leave their husbands. Rather they are to remain strong in their faith, while respecting their husbands and the social order wherever Christian faith is not compromised. Their missionary strategy is to win over their husbands by winsome conduct (purity and reverence), by inner adornment (rather than ostentation and provocative dress), and by a gentle and quiet spirit.

Timothy is an example of one coming to faith out of a mixed marriage. The implication of his mother being Jewish and a believer and his father a Greek (Acts 16:1) is that his father was not a believer. A mother and a grandmother transmitted faith in that family unit (2 Tim 1:5). The circumstances of Timothy's home of origin may contribute, in part, to Paul referring to him as "my dear son," although he also calls Titus a son in the faith. "Son" was a common designation for a pupil.

B. OPPORTUNITIES

1. Parenting

By creative design, marriage in most cases naturally leads to parenting. How the Old Testament and New Testament view family and child rearing sheds light on the marriage relationship as husband and wife also become father and mother. Researching what the Bible has to say about family is not a major part of this study. Nor is this a treatise on parenting. The focus is on how parenting, as described and instructed, bears on an understanding of marriage. Parenting does affect marriage.

The Old Testament culture gave high priority to producing children. The primary family unit was the extended family, identified as the "father's house," *bayit ab*. The next larger units were clan and tribe. In the concentric pattern of family in the Old Testament, marriage makes up the point of genesis. The meaning of marriage and parenting in that kind of family structure does not readily transfer into the contemporary family makeup. The concept of the nuclear family was not conceivable in that culture. However, we can make several observations.

The family structures observable in the Old Testament were essentially the same as in what we know of Middle Eastern families in those times. In anthropological language, biblical (and Middle Eastern) families were (1) endogamous (marriage is within the clan), (2) patrilineal (descent reckoned by father's line), (3) patriarchal (father is master of his family), (4) patrilocal (when a man marries he brings his wife into his father's family), (5) extended (multi-generational, not nuclear), and (6) polygynous (a man may have more than one wife).[15] The household may also have included slaves. If most or all of these family features are rejected for family values today, of what value, it may be asked, is the Old Testament picture? Further, if heterosexual marriage is integral with a male-centered family structure, on what basis can we insist on heterosexual marriage if we do not also insist on patriarchal-hierarchical familial-marital patterns? This line of reasoning does not take into account the big picture of biblical revelation. It does, however, illustrate the need for caution in extrapolating relevant principles from "the way it was."

Narrative material and wisdom literature offer relevant data. The four-generation family story in Genesis 12–50 "invites comparison with the 'soap operas' of daytime television." (Dearman contends this is not a flippant comparison.)[16] The family history (including marital complexities and irregularities) is anything but idyllic. Through all the rivalry between multiple wives and siblings, favoritism, intrigue, violence, deceit, and sexual compromise this family survived as a family. God's promise to bless all the families of the earth through this family remained in place.

15. Patai, *Sex and Family*, 19–21. (Patai uses the term "polygynous.")
16. Dearman, "Family," 120.

God continued to work with them and through them, and that in itself offers hope for today, with the complexities and tangled webs of family life in modern society. The honest reporting should not lead us to dismiss the possibility of healthy marriage and family.

Proverbs has a great deal to say about mothers and fathers and children. Of note is the fact that Proverbs ignores the marital and parental complications of polygamy. Now it may not have been practiced among ordinary people at that time, but it certainly was present in the royal families. However, there are references to unfaithfulness and nagging. In the poetic parallelism that is common in Proverbs, the many specific references to mothers in the second lines imply that parenting is viewed as a shared responsibility. Although a patriarchal family structure may be assumed, father and mother speak with one voice of instruction and are equally blessed by responsive children. The family picture in Proverbs, with overtones of marital relationships, stands in contrast to either turning over child rearing entirely to wife-mother or to limiting her place to giving birth and taking care of babies.

The New Testament emphasizes the spiritual family but does not depreciate biological family or children. Jesus grew up in a family setting of father and mother and siblings. Luke reports a family tension when Jesus was twelve. We have little evidence of what kind of husband and father Joseph was, but we have no reason to think he was not loving, honorable, and responsible. Jesus's family, before grasping his true identity, shows concern for him. Although Jesus's response to his mother's manipulations at the wedding in Cana seems a bit curt, among his words from the cross we have a tender moment as he connects his mother with "the disciple whom he loved." Jesus showed compassion for the distraught parents of a girl who had died. He sarcastically reprimanded the Jewish leaders for subverting the command to honor father and mother. He not only had time for children, but he also used children as models of trust. The parable of the father and two sons does not mention a mother in the family, perhaps assumed to be no longer living, or it is more likely that since the story is about God as father it intentionally leaves out what could be construed as a female counterpart to God (as in pagan religions of that time). The gospel accounts picture Jesus as supportive of parenting as a usual part of marital life.

An exchange between Jesus and a woman in the crowd in Luke 11:27–28 provides insight into how Jesus viewed women and motherhood compared with common cultural values. The woman broke in with, "Blessed is the womb that bore you and the breasts that nursed you." Jesus said in reply, "Blessed rather are those who hear the word of God and obey it." The fact that Jesus's cryptic response seems to be unappreciative of the compliment paid to his own mother prompts a second look. Chantal Logan notes, "Jesus, contrary to Muhammad and almost all cultural patterns, does not sing the praises of motherhood. Yet he does praise women, but on the basis of their character or their faith, not their ability to produce children . . . a woman's value is not tied to her ability to give birth."[17] She goes on to note that this is extremely good news to barren women and to those who have remained single by necessity, or by choice. Jesus's response here is in the same vein as his response regarding his mother and brothers in Luke 8:19–21. Neither time did Jesus depreciate parenting and family while pointing to higher kingdom values.

The Household Codes include child-parent relationships alongside wife-husband relationships. Ephesians 6:1–4 quotes the command to honor father and mother. The inclusion of both parents seems significant in a culture ruled predominately by fathers. Although the New Testament does not put high priority on reproduction and specifically endorses singleness and celibacy, it nevertheless assumes children to be regularly a part of marital and family life. The advice of Jeremiah to the exiles in Babylon to build homes, marry, and have children as part of life that goes on seems to hold in the time of the early church as well. The motive of perpetuating a family name and heritage is notably missing in the New Testament, but the maternal-paternal instincts are also deemed well and good in the kingdom of Christ.

In the New Testament, the spiritual family has priority over the biological family but does not replace it. In 1 Timothy 5, Paul expects the extended biological family to do what it can to take care of widows, before the church family gives assistance. The church family adds a layer to the marriage covenant, providing support and accountability. The church as family is perhaps the dominant image in the New Testament. To the extent that the church as family moves toward women having equality in the church, it follows that that equality should also be experienced in home and family.

---

17. Logan, "Is the Gospel Good News?," 149.

The Scriptures seem to assume that parenting normally is carried out by two biological parents (male and female, in a marriage relationship). Several exceptions show up in the Old Testament. No mention is made of a man being involved in the parenting of the sons of Lot's daughters. Except for the involvement of his biological mother in his infancy, Moses was reared by Pharaoh's daughter, with no mention of a male counterpart. Eli seems to have provided the parenting for Samuel, with minimal contact by his mother. An aunt of Joash (Jehoash), Jehoshabeath (wife of the priest, Jehoiada), rescued him in his infancy and kept him hidden for six years. Presumably she was his primary parent during that time, along with a provided nurse, although her husband is included in the "them" with whom Joash remained during those years (2 Chr 22:12). These several examples have implicit irregularities in them. No examples of same-gender parents are found, although the silence does not prove there were none. The intended norm for parenting is unquestionably clear.

Although the New Testament does not address the matter of single-parent families directly, it certainly does not counter the contention of sociologists that children growing up without both mother and father in general do less well in almost all ways. Yet in 2006, up to a third of parents in the United States were single, mostly female. The percentage of single male parents is on the increase. A further complicating factor is that the census figures do not take into account that single parents may (and in many cases do) have an adult partner living with them, though they are not married. The implications of this scenario for understandings of marriage should be obvious. Except when one parent has died, this problematic situation is tied to either marriage experiences or attitudes toward marriage or both. Sociologists are concerned about what this trend holds for the future, and the church should be also. The church family cannot fully replace a missing parent but can as extended spiritual family provide models and relational support for these children and the single parent.

Although instructing children in the ways of the Lord is a shared responsibility of both mother and father, fathering carries a unique call in representing God as Father, and in being the kind of father God is, to some degree. Therefore, fathering deserves particular attention in consideration of the parenting opportunities.

As noted earlier, a disturbing feature of the current family scene is the growing absence of fathers. This abdication of fathering responsibility following insemination (termed "the male problematic" by Don Browning and others) is not evident in the biblical record. Fathers are prominent and visible in the story, but not to the exclusion of mothers.

Intimations of God as "father" occur in the Old Testament, perhaps more as metaphor than as title. For example, Deuteronomy 32:6, "Do you thus repay the LORD, O foolish and senseless people? Is he not your father, who created you, who made you and established you?" Psalm 103:13 says, "As a father has compassion for his children, so the LORD has compassion for those who fear him." And Jeremiah 3:19b says, "And I thought you would call me, my Father, and would not run from following me." Jesus then commonly addressed God as "my Father" and taught disciples to pray: "Our Father . . ." The gospels retain the Aramaic word "Abba," the common term children first used to speak to their fathers ("Daddy," in English). James includes three references to God as Father. In both testaments God as Father (both in title and imagery) connotes kindness and tenderness. As similarly in the marriage analogy, human experience opens the way to understanding and experiencing God. Jesus assumes the character of human fathers/parents (though evil) to give good gifts to their children to affirm that even more so the heavenly Father gives good things to his children (Matt 7:9–11).

A connection between God as Father and human fathering cannot be ignored. Because of that association, one's perception of God is colored by one's experience with a human father. But that is not a constructive association for many. Viewed positively, human fathers are presented with a challenging opportunity. If healthy fathering is not learned from biological fathers, Jesus's revelation of God as Father sets the model.

A text sometimes brought into service as establishing the connection between "Father" and "father" is Ephesians 3:14–15. Several versions translate *patria* in the second clause as "paternity" or "fatherhood." Most versions have "family." The word is derived from *patēr*, the basic word for "father" in Greek. This is the only occurrence of the term in the New Testament (in singular). In the LXX (where it is found ten times in singular), it is never used to denote the abstract concept of "fatherhood." It always means a specific group of people—family, clan, tribe, or nation. Therefore, this text makes a connection between God as Father and family and parenting through word origins, but usage does not support a distinct parallel connection between "Father" and "fatherhood."

However, this does not eliminate a significant association. Human fathers are representatives of God, along with mothers (as the commandment to honor father and mother implies). And it can be rightly said that a human father is not in a position to be "father" unless he knows the "Father," experientially. This perspective can be upheld without going to the extent of extrapolating a paternalistic construct of marriage from it. That is to say, it is both possible and true to biblical usage to speak of God as "he" and as "Father" and to promote an essential mutuality between husbands and wives and between fathers and mothers as parents.[18]

Robert M. Hicks contends that "the ideal of husband as the singular head of the home is a myth. It is not valid in principle except where the male is a single father."[19] He calls for husbands/fathers to be responsible, but that does not translate into authoritarian control. Among the radical feminists are those calling for a genderless society and family in which the concept of fatherhood has no place. Gynocentric feminism goes even farther in that direction. (Chapter 6 in *From Culture Wars to Common Ground*, Don Browning, et al., reviews the range of feminists' views.)

2. Witness

The contemporary disarray of marriage and family calls for conscious demonstrations of God's intent and grace. The Bible does not make a big point of the witness opportunities of exemplary marriages. We have noted the admonition in 1 Corinthians 7:13–16 that a newly believing spouse is not to initiate separation from an unbeliever, leaving open the positive effect the ongoing relationship could have on the unbeliever.

In Titus 2 the message for the several categories of persons is not fully parallel with the Household Codes elsewhere. The implied context is congregation rather than household. The traditional hierarchical family structure of the surrounding culture is assumed to be appropriate for believers. However, the motivation for proper Christian behavior is relevant for the witness of Christian marriage in the world. Negatively it is "that the word of God not be discredited." Stated positively (in the word to slaves) it is "that in everything they may be an adornment of the doctrine of God our Savior." The last part of the chapter focuses on grace.

---

18. See Miller, *Calling God "Father,"* for his argument that being "father" means being "head." See also Don Browning's response in *Does Christianity Teach?* (which includes a chapter by Miller).

19. Hicks, *Christian Family*, 63.

Jesus's words about love and unity are primarily directed to the community of disciples rather to married couples. However, with key words in a theology of marriage being love (with emphasis on giving rather than getting) and oneness (*henosis*), Jesus's comments on the witness effect are also apropos of marriage. "By this everyone will know that you are my disciples if you have love for one another" (John 13:35). In his prayer, "I in them and you in me, that they may become completely one, so that the world may know that you have sent me and have loved them even as you have loved me" (John 17:23).

The self-serving, throw-away world may get the message, if it is clear. But the figures do not indicate that church-connected "Christians" are doing any better at marriage than the general population. It need not be so.

7

Comparisons

ACQUAINTANCE WITH THE COMMON attitudes and practices associated with marriage in the surrounding cultures of Hebrew and early Christian peoples helps to explain some of the biblical narrative and the strong denunciations of behaviors that do not belong with the people of God.

Although the biblical picture reflects some elements of the cultural context in which the biblical story unfolds, some of the views and practices of marriage in the Bible stand in notable distinction compared with those of the Near Eastern culture in Old Testament times (and even prevailing in varying degrees today) and the Greco-Roman culture of New Testament times. The similarities help in understanding the descriptions of marriage in the Bible. The differences accentuate the uniqueness stemming from an unfolding divine revelation.

A. CULTURES SURROUNDING THE OLD TESTAMENT

Family structures have a bearing on marriage. We noted the features of Middle Eastern families earlier, as identified in anthropological language (endogamous, patrilinear, patriarchial, patrilocal, entended, and polygynous). A full complement of these cultural traits is unique to the Middle East, and they have been the practice in that culture for millennia. The biblical accounts indicate similar patterns. The people in the biblical narrative were part of the broader culture to a large extent. Some of the exceptions and movements within God's covenant people have also been noted above.

If most or all of these family features are rejected for family values today, of what value is the Old Testament picture, it may be asked. Further, if heterosexual marriage is integral with a male-centered family structure, on what basis can we insist on heterosexual marriage if we do not also insist on patriarchal-hierarchical familial/marital patterns? This line of reasoning does not take into account the big picture of biblical revelation. It does illustrate the need for caution in extrapolating relevant principles from "the way it was."

In the Code of Hammurabi, from eighteenth century BC Mesopotamia, one of the great law codes of history, some sixty of the laws (about one-fourth of the whole code) are devoted to strengthening marriage and family. Penalties for adultery are severe. Israelite laws do not stand alone in prescribing faithfulness in marriage and honoring covenant marriage, although not as extensive as in the Hammurabi Code.

The biblical records reflect several additional marriage practices of early cultures. One is marriage by capture. Cultures in which girls were considered a liability sometimes resorted to infanticide. With a resultant shortage of girls for marriage, they then raided other tribes for wives. (The biblical accounts include child sacrifice but not the disposing of unwanted girl babies.) Deborah's song has a line about women as the spoils of war (Judg 5:30), and Deuteronomy 21:10–14 specifies the rules for taking wives as the spoils of war. Another practice in the Middle East is marriage by purchase. It is designated variously as dowry, bride price, or marriage present. The Hebrew word *mohar*, when used in connection with marriage, implies a gift, perhaps remuneration, but not exactly as a purchase.[1] Other Hebrew vocabulary also implies a transfer from father of the bride to the groom, but not as a commercial transaction. For example, Rebekah seems not to have been considered as chattel. Her consent was asked for and given. The practice of the Hebrews connotes more of a respect for personhood than is true in most of the surrounding cultures.

Fertility and progeny were high priority for the Hebrews, along with the Canaanites. The Hebrews were attracted to the fertility rites as they came into Canaan. Although certainly not free from cultic prostitution and religious sexual acts, the Hebrew theology in no way supported fertility rites. Canaanite practices were based on the perception of sexual relations between the gods and goddesses. The Hebrew God had/has no counterpart or consort.

An American archeologist, William G. Dever, argues in his 2005 book, *Did God Have a Wife? Archeology and Folk Religion in Ancient*

---

1. See Janzen, *Exodus*, 305–6.

Israel, that although the Old Testament writings do not depict Yahweh as having a female counterpart, the common folk religion likely included that perspective. He contends that although Asherah usually refers to a pole or tree as part of cultic practices, at times it identifies a female goddess (e.g., 1 Kgs 18:19, with reference to the prophets of Asherah). The biblical accounts indicate an ongoing religious syncretism that included pagan views of deity. But common practices are not the basis for revealed theology.[2]

Since marital issues are front and center with the prophet Hosea, some acquaintance with the marriage customs of that era can be helpful. Extensive research has been done in ancient Near Eastern texts (ANET). None of the extra-biblical material comes out of the time and place of Hosea in the Northern Kingdom. However, neighboring societies of that time were concerned with describing and regulating marriage. Their basic concerns were similar to those of the Hebrews. The assumptions about marriage, adultery, and divorce evident in Hosea were also shared by other cultures.

Allen R. Guenther lists seven marriage concerns found in ANET: "(1) the economic aspects of the marriage agreement, (2) the nature of the marriage arrangement, (3) the conditions under which the marriage would be regarded as broken or severed, (4) the status of children, and their rights of inheritance, including the children of blended families, (5) exceptional or unusual aspects of a given marriage, (6) the consequences of severing the marriage relationship, and (7) the role of family or community in assuring justice and protecting the rights of the weaker parties, usually those of the women and children."[3] The Hebrew laws addressing the same concerns are to be found in Exodus 21–22; Leviticus 18–21; Numbers 27, 30, 36; and Deuteronomy 21–25.

B. Cultures Surrounding the New Testament

Several strands of the Greco-Roman culture of New Testament times need to be set alongside the values and teachings of the Christian movement. One strand has the label the "honor-shame code," perhaps out of military respect for dominance and submission. In simplified terms, honor came through winning and shame or dishonor through losing. Men were

---

2. For a critique of Dever's book, see Ahituv, "Did God Really?," 62–66.

3. Guenther, *Hosea, Amos*, 393. Guenther also lists studies relevant to marriage.

shamed if their space was challenged or lost. The code allowed a double standard, in that if a man could invade another man's space without getting caught, it counted as honor. For women shame was considered a virtue. In the Roman Empire, women gained considerable freedom, becoming more involved in social, economic, and political life. Among the believers in several cities visited by Paul in Macedonia were a number of "prominent women."

Another strand in Hellenized Roman culture, highlighted by Don S. Browning, et al., was the influence of Aristolelian patterns. In *Politics* and *Nicomachean Ethics*, Aristotle delineated how the man of the house is to rule. He called the rule of a master over his slaves as "tyrannical," the relation of husband to wife as "constitutional aristocracy," and the father's relation to his children as "monarchial rule." In respect to husband and wife he said, "For although there may be exceptions to the order of nature, the male is by nature fitter for command than the female."[4] His household rules address the same relationships as those in the New Testament epistles. That raises the question of the source of the New Testament Household Codes. Were they borrowed from Aristotle, Stoicism, or Hellenistic Judaism (with examples in Philo and Josephus)? Or do they simply reflect the accepted contours of the traditional mores of the culture of the day?

Although the New Testament Household Codes are in some respects similar to non-biblical relational lists, the differences do not at all point to a borrowing by the New Testament writers. After showing substantive and radical differences from Greek or Jewish sources and dismissing that the New Testament writers borrowed this tradition from each other, John H. Yoder concludes: "The only remaining source we very logically suspect is that somehow this tradition comes from Jesus."[5]

Mythology makes up part of the backdrop of the New Testament writings. Particularly strong in Asia Minor, the pagan religions centered on goddesses such as Artemis, Cybele, and others that were associated with Eve. In Egypt it was the goddess Isis. The mythologies rewrote the biblical accounts of Genesis, making the female as the primal source of life. Early Gnostic views, with some Jewish Diaspora perversions, are a large part of the religious paganism of the first century. Gender reversals and snake/

4. As cited by Browning, *Culture Wars*, 144.

5. Yoder, *Politics*, 182.

Satan worship added to the myths referred to in the pastoral epistles and the letters to the seven churches in Revelation. The New Testament was not written in a religious vacuum. Although written largely in a proactive mode, the New Testament teaching regarding sexuality, women, and marriage sets new life and community in Christ into a climate of religious aberrations—not taking them out of the world, but shaping life in the world.

The illuminating research of Richard and Catherine Kroeger reveals a lot of the religious climate into which the gospel was taken in New Testament times. They were primarily interested in discovering the context for texts such as 1 Timothy 2:11–15. The distortions they document have relevance for understanding the immediate culture over-against which other New Testament teaching stands as well.[6]

Albert A. Bell Jr., in *The New Testament World*, in his chapter on Greco-Roman morality and personal relations, notes features of the immoral society in which the early church found itself proclaiming the teaching of Jesus. Roman writers explicitly describe the deviant sexual mores of that time. Bell writes: "How strange [Jesus's] words must have sounded: 'You have heard that it was said, "You shall not commit adultery." But I say unto you that everyone who looks on a woman with lust has already committed adultery with her in his heart' (Matt 5:27–28). Paul's description of the 'degrading passions' and 'every kind of wickedness' among the Romans hits right at the mark once we see from their own records what they were like in this era."[7] In chapters on Greco-Roman religions, philosophies, and society structures, Bell provides further extensive details necessary to understand and appreciate the New Testament writings.[8]

Another aspect of the culture surrounding the New Testament was Rabbinic Judaism. As noted earlier, rabbinic Judaism was and is divided on views of marriage and divorce. The traditional position had been to give men/husbands near absolute power in marriage. In biblical times, that would have been the prevailing Jewish understanding, with some shift among Hillelite rabbis. This provides the backdrop in the Jewish community for the teachings of Jesus, Paul, and others. Some further attempts have been made to move toward alleviating the powerlessness of

6. Kroeger, *I Suffer Not*.

7. Bell, *A Guide*, 244.

8. Another source for understanding the biblical context is Campbell, *Marriage and Family*.

women/wives. But the efforts fall far short of equality. "In liberal communities the bride and groom often write more egalitarian *ketubot* (marriage contracts) that reflect their goals for the marriage—either in place of or in addition to the traditional *ketubah*. Both liberal and some traditional Jews may include a prenuptial agreement in their *ketubah* that would require the groom to give the bride a *get*, or Jewish bill of divorce, should the marriage end."[9]

C. NEW TESTAMENT HOUSEHOLD CODES IN CULTURAL CONTEXT

The New Testament Household Codes can be seen as supporting the traditional paternalism of the surrounding culture, or at least not flatly countering it. However, it is seldom noted that the New Testament approach to slavery may be parallel to the emerging view of male-female relations in the Christian community. The New Testament does not openly attack the imbedded institution of slavery. Rather, by telling Philemon to accept his slave, Onesimus, as a fellow human and as a brother in the Lord, Paul addressed the heart of the issue for believers. To be sure, it took centuries for the Christian church to apply that radical perspective. In similar fashion, the New Testament can be seen as radically challenging the prevailing culture's view of women by putting the male-female/husband-wife relationship in christological context, a new level. Both slavery and male domination the New Testament present a trajectory in the application of the gospel.[10]

Mary Stewart Leeuwen has put it this way: "Just as Paul does not call for the sudden overturning by Christians of slavery as an institution, but undermines it from within by urging both slaves and master to treat each other as brothers in Christ, so too for the sake of social order and successful evangelism he advises the recipients of his letters to play along with some of the local norms of patriarchy even as he proclaims that in Christ, 'There is no longer Jew or Greek, there is no longer slave or free, there is no longer male and female; for all of you are one in Christ Jesus' (Gal 3:28). . . . The barriers between Jew and Gentile, slave and free, male and

9. Lamm, "Explaining the *ketubah*," 1.

10. I am using the imagery of trajectory in the sense of the affirmations of the gospel pointing to the working out of the gospel in degrees, which challenged the cultural status quo while still living within the culture. I am not hereby accepting the views of trajectory hermeneutics.

female are to come down, as we are together to be 'heirs of the gracious gift of life' (1 Peter 3:7)."[11]

Although American Christians may generally assume that slavery is a thing of the past, slavery continues in large numbers in the present century. "The U.S. State Department estimates that 17,500 new slaves are brought to the United States every year. . . . One of the biggest hurdles, abolitionists say, is overcoming the general notion that slavery no longer exists. . . . Modern-day slavery looks different from the plantation model most Americans think of when we hear the word."[12] It's a matter of people being forced into doing labor and services for which they are not compensated. The majority of the enslaved today are women and children who are forced into prostitution. This is the reality despite Great Britain abolishing slavery early in the nineteenth century, the United States fighting the Civil War (at least in part over the issue of slavery), and the United Nations prohibiting slavery in 1948. Sadly, it has taken many Christians many centuries to reject human slavery. Yet when they take seriously that Paul told Philemon to accept his slave Onesimus as a beloved brother in Christ, they can readily see that this gospel reality cuts the nerve of the notion and practice of one human being owning and using another human being.

While some Christians have embraced the gospel trajectory of equality in marriage, paternalistic and hierarchical patterns continue in the present. When a man, with notions of innate male superiority, refuses to take directives from, say, a female service representative or physical therapist, because she is a woman, and his wife is able to stand her ground, that marriage is set for tension and competition for control. In both of these issues the gospel of Jesus Christ has not permeated the contemporary culture to the extent that it should. This is not because the gospel has failed but because stewards of the gospel have buried it rather than applying it.

Having reviewed the cultural context of the New Testament Household Codes, we now turn to Colossians 3:18—4:1 as representative of the several New Testament passages of this nature. I am indebted to the astute observations and analysis of Susanne Henderson for the way she has connected the dots in her exegesis of this text. Without getting into an

---

11. VanLeeuwen, "Equal Regard," 21.

12. Haught, *Religious News Service, MWR*, 3.

argument of whether the writer of Colossians incorporated the domestic patterns of Aristotle or some other contemporary sources, it is fair to say that these verses reflect, and on the surface accept, the societal construct of that time. They do not openly repudiate the prevailing hierarchical and paternalistic views of the day. But as we will see, that does not mean wholesale approval of the traditional relational assumptions of the society in which Christians found themselves.

Immediately preceding, as a summary of 3:1–16 and a bridge into the household relational instructions, we have the comprehensive perspective in verse 17: "And whatever you do, in word or deed, do everything in the name of the Lord Jesus . . ." This framework of the lordship of Christ establishes the tone and motivation implicit in "as is fitting in the Lord" (v. 18), "acceptable duty in the Lord" (v. 20), and "fearing the Lord" (v. 22), plus "Lord" three more times and "Master" (*kyrios*). The commonly assumed hierarchy in household relationships is thus placed within a new rank of authority, that of Jesus Christ as Lord.

Noting which party is addressed first in each of the three pairs of instruction yields further evidence of an effort to "Christianize" the Household Codes. In each case the supposed weaker party/parties are addressed as though they have a choice in the matter, making the responses of "be subject to" and "obey" voluntary dispositions. As a counterpart, the instructions to the supposed superior parties do not call for asserting authority, but for tempering their culturally imputed power: "love your wives and never treat them harshly," "do not provoke your children," "treat your slaves justly and fairly, for you know you have a Master in heaven." These features lead Henderson to conclude: "The writer takes the prevailing cultural worldview—that of a fixed household hierarchy—and refracts it through the authority of a Lord who transforms human authority."[13]

Contrary to the view that this pericope was borrowed and placed randomly where it is in the letter, the literary context reveals further interpretative connections. Alongside the positive appeal to "live your lives in [the Lord], rooted and built up in him" (2:6), we find an extended warning not to be driven by "human tradition" and the "elemental spirits of the universe." Chapter 2 identifies these *stoicheia* as seductive human regulations that enslave and divide, the opposite of God's goal of reconciliation, release, and renewal in Christ. These codifications, closely associated with

13. Henderson, "Taking Liberties," 425.

the "principalities and powers," have been disarmed in the cross and are perishing, not eternal. As we connect the dots in Colossians, the societal relational rules of the day reflected in 3:18—4:1 are seen as a case in point of structures of domination that are not in accord with new life in Christ. The christological ethics, applied predominately to relationships, spell out life for those who have been raised with Christ. The qualities listed are apropos of household life.

When we note what follows, in 4:2–6, we may see support for generally respecting society's values so as not to be offensive to the larger community. But even stronger is the calling to positive witness in word and deed to the free realignment of life, including household life, under the lordship of Christ

Dr. Henderson brings together the passage's historical, christological, and literary contexts with interpretative integrity. She asks that as faithful readers of this Household Code we ask ourselves: "Do our homes promote division, discord, and condemnation by 'promoting self-imposed piety' (Col 2:23) that reflects the brokenness of our world? Or do they serve as the staging place for the renewal of that 'old self with its practices' (Col 3:9) bearing living witness to the reconciling marks of 'compassion, kindness, humility, meekness, and patience' (Col 3:12)."[14]

D. ISLAMIC VIEWS ON MARRIAGE

A comparison of biblical views (notably New Testament) with Islamic views of marriage is of value, even though the Qur'an comes centuries later than the Bible. Although proscribing a few elements of the prevailing culture, the Qur'an does reflect much of the traditional Near Eastern culture of many centuries. In many respects the tenets are closer to the Old Testament than to the New Testament. For example:

1. Polygamy is accepted, specifically polygyny (multiple wives) but not polyandry (multiple husbands). Having four wives is to be the maximum, although Muhammad had more than that.

2. Patriarchy defines home rule, with evidence of double standards in which men have more liberty than women. The Qur'an says: "Men are the protectors and maintainers of women, because Allah

14. Ibid., 431. See my comments on the Household Codes in relation to Colossians 3:18—4:1, and essays on "Ethical Lists" and "Elements of the Universe" in *Colossians/ Philemon*. See Swartley, *Slavery*, for more on how the Bible intersects with these issues.

has given the one more (strength) than the other, and because they support them from their means. Therefore the righteous women are devoutly obedient, and guard in (the husband's) absence what Allah would have them guard. As to those women on whose part you fear disloyalty and ill-conduct, admonish them (first), (next), refuse to share their beds, (and last) beat them (lightly); but if they return to obedience, do not seek against them means (of annoyance); for Allah is Most High, Great (above you all)."[15] While adultery is punishable for both men and women, men may have sex with the female slaves in their possession, without blame.[16]

3. Marrying "unbelievers" (those not Muslim) is prohibited, along with giving girls in marriage to "unbelievers."[17]

4. There is to be no pre-marital sex (fornication).[18] There is no dating. Families are involved in arranging marriages, but not against the wishes of the girl.

5. Divorce is permitted for men, with some requirements, but remarriage to the same woman is limited to two times.[19]

6. Slavery (of both male and female) is assumed possible, with the likely source being captives in warfare (warfare being another accepted possibility). Female slaves should not be forced into prostitution if they desire chastity.[20]

7. Marital love is a provision of Allah. "Among His Signs is this, that he created for you mates from among yourselves, that you may dwell in tranquility with them, and He has put love and mercy between your (hearts): verily in that are Signs for those who reflect."[21]

Although the Qur'an presents itself as the correction to the falsifications of the Torah and Evangel, and that only the original Arabic text is authentic, additions to the traditions and creative exegesis through the centuries are far from a monolithic interpretation. While defending the

15. Surah 4:34, Ali translation.
16. Surah 23:5, 6.
17. Surah 2:221.
18. Surah 4:2–4.
19. Surah 2:227–33, 236, 237, 241.
20. Surah 24:2–4, 32, 33.
21. Surah 30:21.

Qur'an as the true revelation via the Prophet, parts of Islam have significantly modified the traditional views of women and marriage. The Qur'an itself is seen by scholars as reflecting the complex marital experience of Muhammad himself. That is, the "revelation" was not without an immediate context. Efforts both to hold the line and to accommodate to cultural change have affected how exegetes of the Qur'an have sought to explain the Islamic "holy book." [22] Exegetes of the Bible engage in similar ingenuities to make the texts say what they want them to say!

In many Islamic countries married Muslim women face the fear of becoming divorced, resulting in the loss of their children, and of their husbands taking on another wife. For the yet unmarried, knowing that men have a degree of advantage over them, they do not welcome marriage, resenting the possibility of polygamy and fearful of divorce and abandonment. Yakuta Abdo, who has roots in a traditional Muslim family in Ethiopia, says she "observed that polygamous marriages were not bonded in love, there was no fellowship and heart-to-heart communication between husband and wife when there were several wives. I yearned for a marriage bonded in loving commitment." [23] Later she met Christ and married a Christian man.

Several sources provide help in comparing biblical views of marriage and family with other religions in addition to Islam: Don S. Browning, et al., *Sex, Marriage, and Families in World Religions* and the whole issue of the *Journal of Ecumenical Studies,* edited by Arlene Swindler, on "Marriage in the World Religions."

Wherein the understandings and intent of marriage in biblical revelation differ from those of surrounding cultures, the differences stem from who Yahweh is in relation to his people in the Old Testament accounts. Practices did not always accord with God's revealed will for marriage. In New Testament times, the notable differences stem from the christological base for the marital relationship. As the implications of the new creation in Christ were being integrated into human relationships, the core theological trajectories were in place, although the contextualized teaching did not always rise to the full truth as it is in Jesus.

22. See Stowasser, *Women in the Qur'an,* for a scholarly analysis of the Qur'an and its interpreters, specifically on the issue of women in Islam.

23. In chapter 7 of *Anabaptists Meeting Muslims,* entitled "Is the Gospel Good News for Muslim Women?," Chantal Logan addresses the distinctions between the gospel and Islam with respect to women and marriage. Yakuta Abdo tells her story in the attached response, 152–53.

8

Purposes for Marriage

THE BIBLE POINTS TO a constellation of purposes implicit in God's design and provision for marriage, purposes that offer vision and challenges for every couple anticipating and experiencing marriage. Defining purposes for marriage include:

a. companionship,

b. establishing a basic social unit/family,

c. context for sexual expression,

d. procreation,

e. full-orbed *henosis,* and

f. witness to Christ-church reality.

Marriage comes into the human story with the first pair of humans. The intentional provision of marriage predates the Fall and the effects of sin in the world. Although no texts, other than Genesis 2:18, explicitly specify the divine reasons for the human marriage relationship, an interrelated combination of purposes can be discerned in the biblical revelation.

Howard Charles called attention to six major emphases in biblical revelation regarding sexuality and marriage:

1. People are more than animals. Personhood entails much more than reproduction.

2. Sex and sexuality are good, with maleness and femaleness reflecting a good Creator's design.

3. Sexuality is set in the context of community, with marriage as the "archetype" of community.

4. God intends marriage to be a permanent union of a man and a woman until broken by death.

5. The New Testament sees marriage not merely as an order of creation, but in relation to the kingdom of God.

6. The sex act is posited solely within the context of marriage.[1]

Before identifying the specifics of God's purpose for marriage, we need to step back and reflect on why a man and woman may enter into marriage, what they bring to marriage, and what they have been led to think it is all about. For many couples chemistry and convenience seem to be top motivators. Emotional and physical chemistry are a part of the picture, but there must be more. Convenience can be a positive factor if it is not a matter of escape from undesirable parental relationships. Complementarity that goes beyond a remedy for loneliness is rooted in Genesis 1 and 2 (male and female in the image of God with a mutual assignment, a companion suited for the man). While in the "key of C," covenant and commitment stand out as key factors. Entering into marriage as covenant (as discussed in chapter 4, section B) puts the marriage on the most sacred level. Commitment, which implies intentionality and resolve, puts a primary emphasis on giving more than getting (as we have put agape love in simple terms). The necessary commitment rests on the couple's commonality in relationship with and commitment to Christ.

"Equal-regard" is the marriage concept being promoted by Don Browning and others of the Marriage and Family Project. That term expresses well the mutuality we have found in the biblical design. But rather than basing "equal-regard" on the premise of love your neighbor as yourself (as they do), carefully exegeting Ephesians 5 and understanding agape-love as devoted more to giving than to getting avoids pitting self-fulfillment and self-sacrifice against each other.

The constellation of divine purposes in marriage looks like this:

MARRIAGE IS TO PROVIDE MALE-FEMALE COMPANIONSHIP AND PARTNERSHIP. In Genesis 2:18, the presenting need for making a "woman" is that God saw/said that it is not good for "the man" to be alone. The text then quickly moves beyond male and female as counterparts to a clearly implied marriage relationship (confirmed by New Testament references). It certainly can be argued that male and female distinction is much more

1. Charles, *Opening the Bible*, 50–54.

than biological equipment for reproduction, and that it is in relationship that male and female reflect the image of God (apart from sex or marriage). Humans are not designed for solitary existence but for life in relationship with other humans, involving two genders.

Several tensions need to be respected and maintained in thinking about marriage as male-female companionship. The human need for "intimacy" (not a biblical term, but a current one that is useful) does not require sex or marriage. Nor does it find satisfaction only in cross-gender relationships. While acknowledging all the potentials of marriage as God's answer to loneliness, we cannot go so far as to say that single persons cannot be fully human, or that the unmarried are less than whole persons. Nor can it be guaranteed that marriage will somehow automatically provide for the human need for intimacy. From the accounts of the crucifixion and of post-resurrection appearances, it becomes clear that the female followers of Jesus during his ministry were not limited to the "womanly" tasks of preparing meals. Jesus had occasion for male-female interaction apart from marriage.

The biblical vocabulary and unfolding view of marriage leaves no question but that a basic purpose of marriage is to produce a relationship of companionship and partnership. The overtones are that of complementarity, mutuality, and koinonia. Marriage, in which each mate enables the other to become more of what he/she can be (Gen 2:18; Eph 5:26–27), fulfills the concept of being "co-human," described as "humanity by partnership."[2] Viewed this way, marriage purposes include nothing of exploitation, domination, convenience, having someone to blame, or self-advancement.

MARRIAGE IS TO PROVIDE THE RELATIONAL SETTING IN WHICH EACH PARTNER SANCTIFIES THE OTHER TO BE AND DO ACCORDING TO GOD'S HOLY PURPOSES. Based on what Christ does for the church, sanctifying himself that those given him be set apart for divine purpose, husbands (and we can say the same for wives) give of themselves to make the focus of their love more saintly, more Christlike, in all relationships and kingdom service. Ephesians 5:26–27 sets the tone for this sanctifying opportunity and call. This high purpose leads husbands and wives to ask themselves: "Am I influencing my mate to draw closer to God and to be responsive to the Holy Spirit's guidance and enablement?" How different from what's

2. Barth, *Ephesians 4–6*, 753.

in it for me. As noted earlier, several students of a biblical understanding of marriage put sanctification of the spouse as a primary purpose of marriage. As noted in consideration of 1 Corinthians 7:12–14, a believing spouse provides a sanctifying canopy over spouse and children when the spouse has not yet come to be a believer.

Marriage is to enable the primary social unit as the core of family. Biblical revelation points to and supports the understanding that one cannot be human alone. Personhood can develop only in relationship, in community. Marriage is the basis for family, and covenant marriage is the basic building block for family and community. Such is the Old Testament perspective, affirmed in the New Testament.[3]

The New Testament introduces another set of values, overlaying the strong biological family/clan social structure of the Old Testament. The New Testament does not negate the biological family but gives priority to the spiritual family. Rather than the civil religion contention that strong families make for a strong citizenry and a strong nation, or the idea that strong family units make for a strong church, the New Testament says that the spiritual family is to inform the biological family. The experience of "church" is to shape marriage and family, rather than the other way around. However, not all expressions and experiences of "church" provide a useful model and support for marriage and family as they should.

The New Testament does affirm marriage and family. As noted before, a number of texts speak positively of marriage. Instructions to parents and children stand in the context of being "in the Lord." Romans 1:20 includes those "rebellious toward parents" in the list of reprobate behaviors.

From the New Testament perspective, the spiritual family does not displace but stands alongside the biological family. Only when the biological family is nonexistent or completely non-functional does the spiritual family go beyond supporting to taking the place of the biological family. Because God's design for marriage joins male and female, this primary social unit provides the context for children to discover and develop their sexuality (maleness and femaleness) first of all in the family unit. Parents

---

3. Noting that a discussion of marriage heads several of the New Testament Household Codes, Barth adds: "For the epitome of social life and gravest of all social problems are located in marriage," *Ephesians 4–6*, 753.

who are single, for whatever reason, need to arrange for children to have a primary relationship with a "significant other" of the other gender.

The primary context for the nurture of children is the parental home, where husband and wife teach and demonstrate what God intends about lived faith and relationships. Only a few Christian groups have posited primary responsibility for the nurture of children with the community rather than with the parents. This is not to minimize the supporting and encouraging role of the extended spiritual family, as parent-child dedication services emphasize.

Covenant marriage, based on faithfulness and love, has the goal of mutually enriching each of the marriage partners. When children are part of the family unit, an objective of covenant marriage is to be a setting for personhood to develop and for faith to be transmitted (Deut 6:4–9; Eph 6:4).

MARRIAGE IS TO AFFORD THE CONTEXT FOR SEXUAL EXPRESSION THAT INCLUDES GENITAL SEX. Sexuality, all that is inherent in maleness and femaleness, is as central to who we are as human beings as our being made in the image of God. All interaction between the genders is in a sense sexual expression. But not all aspects of sexual expression are proper outside of marriage. The various aspects of sexuality are all in a continuum, with some clear dividing lines. Some parts of that continuum are uniquely reserved for expression within marriage—those parts involving erogenous-genital stimulation (whether physically or verbally).

The moral boundaries and the definitions of sex have been changing. Affection has come to be a commonly held boundary in deciding about pre-marital sex. Sex has come to be defined narrowly as coital sex, so that anything short of penetration is not sex. (Helpful books include those by Hershberger, Small, Smedes, and Knight.)

As noted earlier, the Scriptures assume that the human sex drive can be controlled and restrained. The Scriptures also assume that the psychosomatic aspects of sexuality are pronounced good and are to be enjoyed within the intimacy of marriage. Although sensualism has become as prominent as violence in our entertainment culture, there is place for a healthy sensuality in the context of marriage. Sex is an interpersonal experience, not simply a physical act and can rightly be regarded as spiritual communion. Some would put this in the language of the mystery of sacramental sex, as a celebration of God's gift of each other.

The descriptive word "sexy," as used in contemporary speech, does not have any counterpart in the languages of the Bible. (The expression "of good appearance" may be an approximation.) Categories under the rubric of "sex" now include premarital sex (rather than the biblical term fornication), extra-marital sex (instead of adultery), fun-sex (sex for pleasure), repro-sex (sex for procreation), and love-sex (sex between persons, whether married or not, who love each other—both heterosexual and homosexual).[4]

Christian teaching needs to recapture the biblical meaning of love-sex, within the lifelong commitment of marriage. The pervasiveness of recreational sex in our culture can be challenged only by accentuating what ought to be true in love and marriage.

MARRIAGE IS TO CONSTITUTE THE INTENDED SETTING FOR PROCRE-ATION. Reproduction is written into the marriage equation from Genesis 1:28 on. Even though part of the original assignment, producing children seems to be the human pattern more out of instinct than out of obedience. Those who were childless were not that way because they wanted to be. An obsession with having posterity at times overrode the intended way of procreation.

The New Testament does not reflect the high priority on fertility (fecundity) that reigned in much of the Old Testament. However, children are highly valued as gifts of God and assumed to be present. There is certainly no support for abortion as convenience, and there is nothing specified about birth control. The choice of celibacy stems from other than limiting pregnancy. The only recorded instance of birth control is Onan's action in Genesis 38:9.

As may be inferred from the previous purpose of marriage, the findings of this study do not support the contention that the only legitimate reason for sex is to produce babies. Yet what was good from creation about male and female being joined, including reproduction, has not changed with kingdom values being overlaid.

The increasing prevalence of women choosing to have babies and raise children without a father in the picture runs counter to the biblical intent. The rationale that they have so much love to give leaves out thoughts and feelings about men and marriage. The idea of a one-gender parental entity (it can hardly be called a social unit) clashes with the

4. See Miller, *Proverbs*, 89–90, for more along this line.

second purpose of marriage, above, and with marriage being the God-intended setting for procreation.

MARRIAGE IS TO INTEGRATE THE FULL SPECTRUM OF SPIRITUAL, SOCIAL, PSYCHOLOGICAL, PHYSICAL, AND SEXUAL ASPECTS OF HUMANNESS. The arithmetic of two becoming one (Gen 2:24; Matt 19:5–6; Eph 5:31) is intended to encompass the whole range of humanness, not only genital union. Marriage is uniquely designed to facilitate a full-scale *henosis*. As noted in the companionship purpose, human needs for companionship and intimacy can be, and are, met in non-marital relationships (both same- and cross-gender). What is special about the marriage provision is that the several aspects of personhood and of maleness and femaleness have an unequaled integration potential. The blending of commonalities and differences, gifts and perspectives, for two growing persons must bring a smile to God's face as he contemplates the possibilities.

MARRIAGE IS TO MIRROR AND EXEMPLIFY THE SPIRITUAL RELATION-SHIP OF CHRIST AND HIS BODY, SPECIFICALLY CHRIST'S LOVE FOR THE CHURCH. In a slightly different but related vein, God wants marriage to direct attention to the wonder of Christ and the church. It is worth saying again that somewhat parallel to Jesus words to the Father, "As you, Father, are in me and I am in you, may they also be in us, so that the world may believe that you have sent me" (John 17:21), we may say, "May husband and wife become one in the love and grace that is in Jesus, so that the world may come to see the spiritual reality of Christ and the church." The witness value of marriages that approach their potential raise the sights well beyond just managing to stay together for life. This perspective also reminds us of the negative witness of marriages that fail and fall short of what they could be. As parents are God's representatives before their children, marriage partners take on the awesome responsibility of reflecting the relationship of Christ and his body, the church

Obviously a division of the purpose of marriage into these seven facets is an arbitrary exercise. However, one value of separating them is to accentuate awareness of how much they are interrelated. The wonder of the meshing of these "planetary gears" emphasizes the wisdom of God's creative-redemptive design.

SUMMARY

Although the social sciences offer much help in reflecting on and "lubricating" the marriage relationship, the focus of this study is on the theological underpinnings of marriage as discerned from biblical revelation. Therefore, we need to revisit the findings and resultant affirmations and identify the theological "whys" of these affirmations. This goes beyond any accumulated wisdom about how to have a better marriage, important as that may be. If we accept the challenge of elevating marriage to a higher plane and promoting the God-intended potential for marriage, the theological base is crucial. Who God is as Creator and Redeemer and the nature of his covenant relationship with humans, culminating in Christ, will need to shape our efforts. As noted earlier, this entails the discipline of a theology of marriage that goes beyond building the case for marriage on a few selected "proof texts." What, then, are the theological bases and understandings of marriage according to biblical revelation?

From Jesus's reference to Genesis 1 and 2 and from the Genesis texts themselves we glean a sense of the intent for marriage "as it was in the beginning."

- Being made male and female "in the image of God" brings the Creator's wise design into the marriage relationship.

- A theology of marriage must take into account a theology of humanness.

- Having "one" covenant God, being promised to "one husband," Christ (2 Cor 11:2), and expressing marriage as becoming "one flesh" highlights both the exclusivity and the wholeness of marriage.

- The close association of Yahweh's covenant with a people, and marriage as covenant with God as witness, elevates marriage above a merely human arrangement.

- The specific references to Christ in connection with marriage establish a christological construct for understanding marriage.

- With some evidence of digression in the Old Testament along with elements of unfolding revelation, the New Testament stands out as both restoration and full revelation of God's word for marriage and related factors.

- The kingdom perspective of the New Testament modifies some understandings of marriage, but the basic factors of fidelity and love that have their roots "in the beginning" continue to shape marriage.

- The motivation of assuring a future through posterity that pervades the Old Testament picture of marriage-family-children is radically modified with the New Testament hope of resurrection.

- The centering in on love as giving more than getting and as demonstrated in God's love/Christ's love injects a theological perspective into thinking about and expressing love in marriage.

- Although coming out of a first-century social context, the New Testament provides a trajectory view of what human relationships can be in the kingdom of Christ, including marital and family relationships

- The biblical paradigm of marriage comes to us in the format of *inclusio,* beginning in Genesis 1 and 2, and ending in Revelation 21 with the marriage of the Lamb and his bride.

- This big picture of the provision for human marriage in the grand design should be the context for considering minimalist questions about what qualifies as marriage.

- The emerging purposes for marriage in God's design all carry theological overtones.

The elements of a biblical construct of marriage that have surfaced in this exploration are not without some remaining questions and tensions. However, they do provide a consistent and holistic basis for teaching, and for building and nurturing marriages to the glory of God in the kingdom of Christ.

9

Challenges and Opportunities for the Church

THE OVERARCHING GOAL OF this inquiry into what needs to be included in a biblical theology of marriage is that the church may become better equipped to uphold God's intent and provision for marriage. The church must speak up with a clear voice. The challenge is a grim scene. Increasing percentages of couples choose to live together without marriage. The numbers of single parents multiply. The boundaries of sex and sexuality have shifted greatly in recent decades. Marriage becomes another illustration of a throw-away culture (dump this one and try for a better one). Some marriages within the church are simply endured, falling far short of their potential—a witness to Christ and the church. The symptoms go on and on. The mounting evidence cannot be ignored that family and marriage are in deep trouble.

On the other hand, plaintive voices cry out that there must be something better than what the rudderless post-modern society has to offer. Some are recognizing the bankruptcy of a culture that has been saying that there are no boundaries, no rules other than doing what comes naturally and what pleases *me*. Having no clue as to how to build a satisfying life, they are open to a proactive initiative from the church. The opportunity is ripe, not to create something new, but to extend the Creator-Redeemer's design and provision.

The aim here is not to outline a full-scale program of teaching and pastoral care with respect to marriage. Rather it is to call attention to the contribution of biblical revelation, the faith factors, so they can become operational in the church's ministry as it responds to the challenges of marriage. Each of the following seven areas will highlight several core theological underpinnings. How these suggested faith factors, and others, are implemented will be up creative local leadership.

A. STRENGTHENING EXISTING MARRIAGES

One facet of the larger picture is to get existing marriages on a more solid base. Just because marriage has been a given in the human race from the beginning does not mean everybody understands and appreciates the intricacies of this *henosis* of male and female. The animal kingdom operates to a large extent on instinct. Some species even show evidence of monogamy and of family structure. Humans do know something about bonding and mating, but it does not seem to be the case that humans instinctively know how to experience a fulfilling marriage. Sexual attraction and wanting to have babies are generally present in the human makeup, but marriage as we find it in biblical revelation does not unfold automatically. Although we are made to be in fellowship with God and fellow humans, sin affects relationships both with God and with each other. Therefore it is incumbent on the church to keep coming back to the basic elements of covenant marriage.

An analogy may highlight the task. As a computer hard drive gets disorganized and compromised by use and misuse and needs to be defragmented and have errors corrected on a regular basis, so marriages need to be realigned with divine purposes from time to time. Both internal and external factors are capable of derailing elements of the relationship.

Particularly among those who maintain strong convictions against divorce, their marriages can become little more than an endurance challenge, maybe considered a "cross" to bear. Marriages that fall far short of their potential leave the partners settling for mediocrity as par for the course. The church needs to raise the bar and provide both challenge and support.

The flip side of putting an emphasis on giving love is that the giver needs to grow in discovering and knowing what gives pleasure and fulfillment to his or her partner. Assumptions do not take into account male-female differences and individual factors. Men in particular, it seems, who have been primarily following their drives may need to be challenged to find out (by asking) and focus on ways of showing love that communicate deeply. This can be a facet of the "knowing" that is integral with marriage. The reward for a husband and for a wife is in the joy of giving in a way that the spouse indeed knows he or she is loved.

An increase of divorces among those married for a number of years calls for reminding married couples of the basics and offering maintenance resources. We cannot assume that if they have made it for twenty or more years that it's a sure thing all the way. Both parenting and experiencing "the empty nest" affect the dynamics of marriage.

With all that needs to be said about mutuality and the shared life, it is not at all unusual for spouses to face the reality that one or the other is no longer able to carry his or her part of the load. Marriage vows may include something about "in sickness and in health," but taking care of a mate who no longer recognizes the one to whom he or she is married tests the depth of the commitment. It also affords an opportunity for the spiritual community to extend support during an ongoing grief experience of progressively losing one's mate.

FAITH FACTORS. The church has an opportunity to expand the vision of marriage potentials. Revisiting the foundations should underscore the multiple dimensions of the marriage covenant and the oneness (henosis) into which the couple has committed themselves to grow. As life circumstances change, the contours of a marital relationship may need to be adjusted and mutually refocused. Christians should think of their marriage as a testimony of grace and as pointing to the wonder of Christ and the church. If husbands (as well as wives) can catch a vision of the humbling challenges in Ephesians 5:21–33, marriage will become an expanding venture. Married couples may need to grow in understanding love (including marital love) as focusing more on giving than on getting. With the sanctification of the spouse being a prime purpose for marriage, that vision can put mediocre, as well as relatively good marriages, on a new and higher plane. The church has a crucial role in helping couples see and experience marriage and family as within the context of the spiritual family and the values of the kingdom of Christ.

Ron J. Sider makes the case that healthy marriages are a significant means for Christians to be demonstrating the gospel in a mixed-up world.[1] The vision is for more than survival in the marital relationship; the world needs to see what the gospel of grace can do. The vision is to utilize healthy marriage as a "tool" of evangelism. But since the divorce rate for professing Christians is almost as high as for those not professing Christian faith, there's nothing automatic in this challenging opportunity.

---

1. Sider, *Doing Evangelism Jesus' Way*, with subtitle *How Christians Demonstrate the Good News.*

B. PREPARATION FOR MARRIAGE

A second major area of opportunity is that of preparation for marriage. The church needs to find creative ways to counteract the ignorance, misconceptions, and distortions regarding marriage prevalent in our culture and particularly in the entertainment industry. Even more important than identifying what is wrong is promoting what is right.

In contemporary word pictures, the comparative views of marriage may be thought of as Velcro, duct tape, or glue. Velcro imagery suggests that the option of easy separation is an intentional part of the design. The duct tape model suggests that although splitting is not easy and may involve some pain, it is possible and leaves few long-term effects. The glue figure conveys that it is known at the outset that this is going to be a permanent, lifelong bond. It needs to be understood up front that covenant violation is sin.

A multi-media approach is called for in teaching young people long before marriage. This may include sessions with the engaged, group settings that include those with exemplary marriages (and those who have worked through rough times), and celebrations of lasting marriages. Marriage needs to be informed and supported by the resources of biblical faith and a caring community, rather than letting it be a do-it-yourself venture.

Living together before marriage has been hailed as a good way to test compatibility, but not according to marriage in biblical revelation. Pastors may find themselves talking with couples who have been sexually active and perhaps living together and now are considering the step of marriage. Here is opportunity to explore with them the depth of marriage oneness (*henosis*) that is not even on the same page as noncommittal sex, why they have chosen the deviant shortcuts, and why there has been resistance to covenant commitment. The compatibility factors that are essential are in personal faith commitment and in value systems (in light of the kingdom of Christ).

The faithful church will do well to give specific attention to "why wait" until marriage. Knowing where the boundaries of healthy moral expressions of sexuality are is crucial, for relationships prior to marriage and within marriage. Unless couples know what their convictions are and why they hold them, they can easily find themselves beyond the point of return—to be regretted later. The popular assumption that it's not sex unless there is penetration needs to be faced honestly. The church needs to help couples set their boundaries based on their faith commitment. [2]

FAITH FACTORS. The biblical understanding of marriage as covenant, with the covenant including God, has conceptual and communication potential. Covenant calls for a higher level of commitment than is true of agreement or contract. Those at the threshold of marriage need to hear that covenant does not include leaving the back door open for easy escape. The oneness (*henosis*) of marriage needs to be envisioned as much more than feelings/chemistry/sex. Although in its early stages marriage holds more of a prospect of getting than giving, the goal of mature love needs to be injected into the picture at the outset. Individual and shared mission in life may get pushed aside in the choice of marriage and marriage partner, unless the church (pastor) intentionally paints kingdom concerns into the picture. A young man shared with a counselor his struggles to know how God wanted him to invest his life. Then he added that while he was waiting to find his particular mission, he was going to get married. The counselor was aghast. This fellow did not know what direction his life was going to take, but he was going to make a lifelong marriage commitment quite apart from his/their mission under Christ.

The vernacular expression "getting hitched" conveys relevant meaning. A team yoked together needs to be going the same direction, with common goals and values. The values factor is crucial and leads right into discussion of kingdom values. Couples will likely need help in recognizing the roots of their value systems (homes of origin, peers, culture) and in assessing how well their value systems overlap and can meld together. This is the gospel agenda.

Values differences and compatibilities show up in the full range of life experiences. In our highly materialistic culture, money management and the relative importance of possessions need to be faced head-on by couples considering marriage. This affords counselors opportunity to inject kingdom values as of higher priority than equaling or reacting to previous life experience. The Bible has much to say about money. Testimonies of those who have struggled with ideals of chastity and virginity are valu-

---

2. Kaufman, *Freedom Fences*, with the subtitle, *How to Set Limits That Free You to Enjoy Your Marriage and Family*, focuses more on marriage than on before marriage, but the engaging discussion of setting boundaries is pertinent in this stage as well.

able for those in the emotionally and hormonally volatile period before the wedding.

The community of faith needs to become a primary source of accountability and support. From a New Testament perspective, the spiritual family stands above the biological family. The "leaving" and "cleaving" factor creates a new social unit. But it is still true that marrying is marrying into a biological family, with whatever complicated relationships that may entail.

The issues are a bit different when one or both persons entering into marriage has been previously married. (Remarriage after divorce is addressed in section E, below.) Here we are thinking about a previous partner having died. What a couple brings to marriage will be different if one has experienced married life and the other not. If it's a widow and a widower, their backlog of experience will not be identical. Comparisons are inevitable, and the degree of previous satisfaction will affect anticipations and adjustments.

These, and other, variables need to be included in premarital counseling. Depending on their stage of life, companionship and convenience may be leading purposes for marriage. The value systems and life goals of each one need to be openly and honestly explored. Pastors will have opportunity to explore with them the relevant biblical faith factors, and because of the prior experience factor, to do so at an existential level that dreamy-eyed first-timers find harder to grasp.

C. STRESSED MARRIAGES

A third area is ministry with those whose marriages are stressed. When a marital relationship comes upon hard times, stormy times, a couple may need help in reviewing the basis for their marriage. What divergent views of sexuality and male-female relationships have they brought to their marriage? What faith factors have they built into their marriage? Which ones have they undervalued or neglected? A crucial question is, where is Jesus in this relationship? If they find they have grown apart, what interests and influences have become wedges? Many factors in life experience contribute to persons changing over the years, likely in different directions—children, work/careers, financial stress or abundance, health, and social opportunities. They may need help in identifying their commonalities and core values. The individualism of the world culture needs to be curbed to achieve the potentials of togetherness.

When life is not unfolding the way it was dreamed to be, for one or both partners, they could use help in looking honestly at why they are having second thoughts about marriage. The agenda could well include reviewing their marriage trail thus far, rechecking their life values, and getting in touch with what they brought to marriage out of their homes of origin (assumptions and reactions). The needed help may go beyond the competency of the pastor.

Faith factors. Appreciating marriage as a covenant, and addressing problems within that understanding, can provide some needed objectivity. Depending on the causes of marital stress, relevant factors may include: mutuality, a love that majors in giving more than getting, grace for forgiveness and reconciliation and healing, and seeing the big picture in which there's more to it than one partner's subjective sense of fulfillment. With Jesus and his kingdom in the picture, it is presumptuous to pre-limit the Lord's resources for regaining (or perhaps beginning to achieve) a healthy marital relationship.

Depending on where the marriage bond is being challenged, a guided examination of Ephesians 5:21–33 may be helpful. What does it mean to "submit to one another out of reverence for Christ"? The passage has a good bit more to say to husbands than to wives, although if written for our culture, the weight might shift. For some couples, 1 Corinthians 7:1–5 could bring a more balanced perspective. Most times priorities will be a key factor. The New Testament emphasis on kingdom values and goals needs to be heard. Reviewing the constellation of purposes for marriage, and which ones have been integrated into their marital life, may be helpful.

While grace is a key factor, we ought not to be so given to grace that repentance and change are glossed over. There is no substitute for honesty, with each other and with God. The human tendency to assess blame easily results in ducking personal responsibility in achieving healthy relationships. Gary Thomas observes: "Couples don't fall out of love so much as they fall out of repentance."[3]

---

3. Thomas, *Sacred Marriage*, 96.

D. FAILED MARRIAGES

A fourth area of opportunity and responsibility for the church is to relate to those whose marriages have failed. Whether through infidelity or choice (by either partner) to apply the resources of faith and community, some marriages come to a point of being beyond repair. If they could reattach, it would be essentially a new beginning.

The reality of divorce means the undergirding marriage theology will need to be "bilingual." It must address the needs of marriages that are intact and be there for those whose marriages have crashed. A redemptive approach toward those with broken marriages does not lower the standard, as has sometimes been feared and argued. The church can both take an initiative in teaching and promoting lifelong covenantal marriage and give blessing to remarriage after divorce. (More below.) It is not doublespeak but upholding the gospel in all its richness.

The breakdown of a marriage calls for discerning what fundamental faith factors were not operative. Another task is to get in touch with the resources of biblical faith for going on with life. Because there are so many variables in the demise of a marriage, the intersection of faith factors and life experience must be contextualized. There may or may not be opportunity to relate to both persons. The church with opportunity to relate may not have had previous contact with these persons.

FAITH FACTORS. Grace is a key ingredient for divorcees in finding inner healing. Divorce is not pleasing to God, but divorce is not unpardonable. Each partner needs to accept his or her own responsibility, neither more nor less. With the aid of a competent listener, persons will need to come to an honest assessment of what went wrong with the marriage. Forgiveness will be a necessary step toward emotional and spiritual well-being. The capacity to forgive stems from getting in touch with God's forgiveness in Christ. Feelings of anger will likely need to be faced. All of the emotional and spiritual agenda of profound loss prompts each person to revisit the goals and purpose of life. Whether or not another marriage is in the picture, the life agenda is that of rebuilding. A support group, perhaps identified as an accountability group, can provide a safe setting (not unlike a cast on a broken limb).

The helpfulness of a faith community in times of the trauma of divorce will depend on how well the gospel of grace, compassion, and hope has been integrated into the corporate psyche. The faith community may be frustrated by the distancing of at least one of the parties going through a divorce. If they both continue to relate to the congregation, the congregation will likely need help in avoiding the blame game and polarization.

Writing for pastors and congregations, George R. Ewald calls for both a theology of marriage and remarriage and a theology of failure. Among the practical suggestions for ministry is a "Service of Closure."[4] A divorce recovery group, with church sponsorship, can open doors to the many persons around with fractured marriages.

E. REMARRIAGE

Remarriage after the death of a spouse (whether the experience of one or both persons anticipating marriage) provides an opportunity to review the basics of marriage. Previous experience does not guarantee clear theological understandings.

When remarriage is being considered following divorce (for either or both partners), a number of issues should be faced with the help of a competent counselor. Questions include: What have I learned? What resources do I plan to make use of this time?

When one partner has had previous marital experience and the other has not, another layer is added to the home-of-origin factor. Awareness of what each person is bringing to the marriage needs to be shared openly— expectations, fears, and more or less fixed patterns of life. In every case, it is a new beginning.

FAITH FACTORS. Persons considering remarriage would do well to review understandings of biblical teachings on divorce and remarriage and have opportunity to process any questions they may have. A divorcee should get into structured reflection on how this new marriage will be different. Is there an unresolved/unfinished agenda to be addressed before moving on? Again, it is well to remember that we should not be so given to grace that repentance/change is not faced honestly. The challenge is to plan and strive for a marriage that will give witness to the love and grace of Christ. Reviewing the basic elements of marriage for Christians (for example, the purposes and summary, found in chapter 8) can give the couple opportunity to consciously identify factors they find Christ calling them to build into this new relationship.

---

4. Ewald, *Jesus and Divorce*, 125–29.

F. SINGLE ADULTS

A sixth area is in relating to single adults. Perhaps this area should have headed the list. Inclusion is more than oh by the way, let's not forget our single people. Ministry in this area also calls for sensitive balance in what is said and implied. This means guarding against having persons who are single (whether by choice or not) get the impression that they are second class when the church is voicing the lofty ideals and potentials of marriage.

The percentage of single persons is rising in America. More are choosing to marry later in life, or not at all, or to stay single after divorce or the death of a spouse. There are valid reasons for staying single, of course, but for some the choice is a reaction to what they see in some of the marriages around them. They find themselves thinking, *If that's what married life is like, who needs it?* The unmarried persons among us are a major challenge for the church—not to try to get them married, but to be the presence of Christ in a diverse and sometimes confused culture.

FAITH FACTORS. The number of New Testament followers of Jesus who were single confirms that singleness can be a calling in the kingdom. It can be helpful to affirm that sense of call in those who experience pressure from society or family to get married. They can "be strong in the grace that is in Christ Jesus" (2 Tim 2:1, written by Paul to Timothy, apparently both of them single).

The New Testament perspective that one's future is not dependent on biological posterity, but rests on resurrection, is especially relevant for single persons. It also needs to be heard across the board. Male and female being made in the image of God is about sexuality, but sexuality and sex are not interchangeable terms. Cross-gender fellowship, apart from marriage, affords an answer to human loneliness. This is especially true for life in the spiritual family.

Church groups that want to incorporate single persons into spiritual *koinonia* need to cultivate conversation about life in Christ more than about their children. Single persons need to get a sense that they are in the loop, not out of it.

Cross-gender friendships, where at least one of the "friends" is single, fall under the umbrella of male and female together in the image of God. But cautions on possible relational deficiencies and the reality of hormones are in order. The workplace often offers the circumstances in which affairs come about if due caution is not exercised. In an article "When Friendship Goes Too Far," Gerald W. and L. Marlene Kaufman call attention to the way the unwary can drift into unhealthy cross-gender relationships.[5] *Single Voices* offers stimulating insights for a church composed of both single and married persons to address the issues and needs of singleness within a caring community.[6]

G. SINGLE PARENTS

Persons become single parents for a variety of reasons: unmarried (having adopted a child, sex resulting in pregnancy, in-vitro fertilization), divorced (with child/children), or death of spouse. When the two-parent (m/f) context is not the case, the person with sole parental responsibility cannot provide all that is needed for the child/children. How can children come to healthy sexual identity without the primary unit providing both male and female models and cross-gender experience? Where does a single parent turn when a marriage partner is not in the picture? What are the options when marriage is not the setting for parenting? The contemporary phenomenon of the prevalence of single parents cannot be ignored by the church. This trend reveals underlying attitudes about marriage stemming from negative experience, cultural bent toward independence ("I can do it myself"), or failure of the church to teach and resource the dynamics of parenting. There is no easy fix for this challenge.

Faith factors. The Bible provides very little by way of examples of single parents. In the polygamous families in the Old Testament (such as David and Solomon, and to a lesser extent the patriarchs), although the father was not totally absent, mothers apparently were the primary parents. The New Testament does encourage the involvement of extended family (where that is possible). The spiritual family can step in the gap to some extent, although that does not address some of the root causes of this irregular family structure.

Teaching on God's intent for shared parenting responsibilities needs regular attention. As is the case with broken marriages, the church will need to minister to single-parent families while also upholding the wisdom of God's design for two-parent families. Opportunities for

5. Kaufman, "When friendships go too far," 11–13.

6. Yoder and Yoder, *Single Voices*.

inter-generational activities can enhance the functioning of the spiritual family. *Meditations for Single Moms* speaks to mothers parenting alone.[7] Resources are also needed for single dads.

H. A FURTHER NOTE ON CROSS-GENDER FRIENDSHIPS

Relationships are essential for personhood. In that the image of God entails human beings being male and female, cross-gender relationships are not limited to marriage. The mysteries of sexuality are a fact of life both within and beyond marriage. The human need to love and be loved and for degrees of intimacy find fulfillment outside of and beyond the primary marital and family relationships. (Human relational needs are also met in same-gender associations and friendships.) Modern workplaces often have built-in situations where cross-gender friendships may develop and grow. In reality, married persons may spend as much or more time with persons of opposite gender as with their spouses. Since the fruitful possibilities come with predictable hazards, cross-gender friendships call for eyes-open caution. The potentials are complicated further by the likelihood that both persons are not at the same comfort level in relational expressions (e.g., touch). Other variables include marital status and Christian commitment.

Guidelines for healthy cross-gender friendships include:

- Maintain openness and honesty within the friendship and particularly with spouses.

- (For the married) Give special time and attention to nurturing the marriage relationship.

- Contract accountability with a trusted person(s) within the faith community.

- Keep aware of the dynamics of sexual energy, and avoid potentially compromising situations.

- Establish and respect conscious personal boundaries, and respect community boundaries.

- Value and guard the opportunities for healthy cross-gender spiritual friendships

7. Donoghue, *Meditations*.

Regarding cross-gender spiritual friendships, Wendy M. Wright notes, "Beyond the dangers, there are unexpected rewards." She senses that "such spiritual friendships are best realized between two people who are each otherwise grounded by a successful marriage, a religious community, or of a consciously chosen single lifestyle. If this is not the case, the mutuality and equality of friendship may be hampered."[8]

This study underscores that there is a relevant theology of marriage. Many more of the elements of a biblical understanding of marriage could be included in these several areas. Although the pastoral care persons will have plenty of opportunities to integrate biblical marriage theology into their ministries, a major place needs to be given to the teaching ministry of the church in a variety of settings. Working with groups offers a fruitful approach. May the love of God, the wisdom of Christ, and the power of the Spirit enable the church to rise to the occasion.

WEDDING MEDITATION

(An example of incorporating biblical faith
perspectives into a service of marriage.)

I am a grandfather of the groom. The couple is a year beyond college. About four hundred guests are in attendance. The meditation is to be held to ten minutes. My part in the service is limited to what follows.

So, you two are getting "hitched" today! Now that vernacular expression does have pertinent imagery. For example, as you think of a team yoked together, it takes mutual effort to move forward effectively. For being connected as a team, it's crucial that the two are going in the same direction and have common goals and values. For marriage harmony, it is imperative that the partners have compatible value systems. A clash of value systems has put many marriages on the rocks. Those critical common values worth living by are to be found primarily in Jesus Christ and his kingdom, not in the culture around us.

Let's reflect more about the meaning of marriage. Marriage worthy of the name is much more than "chemistry" and "convenience." Useful concepts and dynamics center on covenant and commitment.

A contract (with small print disclaimers and loopholes) is not an apropos concept. Reciprocity (I'll do for you if you do for me) also falls

8. Wright, "Spiritual Friendship," 21–23.

short of yielding a lasting and fulfilling marriage. The image of Velcro won't do—where the bond is temporary and separation easy and painless. Our throw-away culture has the mentality, "If I'm no longer happy with something, I pitch it and get another—wishfully better." Holding life together with something like duct tape may be a bit stronger but not really intended for the long term. Glue comes closer to God's intent for the human marital bond.

Experiencing marriage as covenant really involves multiple covenants.

The primary covenant is you as husband and wife covenanting with each other. Having this wedding in a worship setting symbolizes that you are also making covenant with God. Then there's the added covenant with family and friends. They are here as witnesses, and they add both resources and accountability. And the state comes into it as well, making it a public and legal commitment.

I know you are aware that I have spent a lot of time exploring a biblical theology of marriage. That stems from the assumption that biblical revelation has a vital message for the confused state of marriage these days. Thank you for your trust in me to hold this meditation to ten minutes—me with a thirty-thousand-word manuscript and a captive audience!

In the Old Testament human marriage is used as the "known" human experience to get God's people to appreciate how their unfaithfulness affected the covenant relationship with God. In the New Testament, things are reversed. The relationship of Christ and his body, the church, is the informing model for human marriage. Mutual submission arises out of respect for Christ. Husbands are to love their wives as Christ loves the church. That's what Ephesians 5 says. This goes way beyond viewing marriage as the expected, traditional thing to do.

The challenge to you, _____ and _____, and for all marriages, is that your marriage be a witness to and demonstration of the love and servanthood exemplified in Jesus Christ. That's a high calling, I know, but our world desperately needs that witness.

Since marriage usually includes also parenting, let me remind you that the fifth of the ten commandments (about honoring father and mother) is closely connected with the previous ones (about God's name and day). This means parents are to be honored because they are representatives of God. Indeed, our perceptions of God are greatly influenced by our human parents. So, any children in your life will primarily learn about God by experiencing you as their parents. I am setting the bar high, I know, and I make no apologies. But think of it as an exciting potential, more than an obligation.

Many sociologists are alarmed at what is happening to family life and marriage in the world in recent times. Troubling factors are threatening what our Creator intended human marriage to be. Divorce rates are going down, primarily because more couples are cohabiting without getting married. Diverse attempts are being made to redefine marriage—not broaden, but redefine marriage. The effects are destructive of family, and children are the tragic losers. When Jesus was questioned about divorce, he focused on marriage, as he put it, "as it was in the beginning," quoting from Genesis 1 and 2.

Commitment speaks of blending the lives of persons with determination to make it work, with the grace of God. The result is greater than the sum of the parts. By the way, the arithmetic is not one-half plus one-half equals one, but one plus one equals one, the mystery of two becoming one in a way that is interpersonal and spiritual, much more than physical.

Since you will each be growing, changing persons, experiencing the oneness of marriage is a moving target. Your commonality needs to be in your commitment to Jesus. Intentionality is a key factor here. Happy, fulfilling marriage is not automatic.

A husband was complaining to a counselor about the miserable person his wife was. The counselor said, "I'm surprised you married such a person," to which the husband responded, "She wasn't that way when I married her." The counselor replied, "Oh, she got that way living with you!"

A serendipitous finding in my biblical study is that love rightly understood means being more devoted to giving than to getting. Of course, there is getting in marriage, but agape love (majoring in giving more than getting) rightly applies to the whole range of expressions of love and affection. The center section of the Scripture read earlier, 1 Corinthians 13, is actually made up of a series of verbs, not adjectives as in most translations. That is to say, love is something you do. We all have a need *to love* as well as *to be loved*.

In recent years, there's been an increase in divorces among those married many years (twenty, thirty, or more years). The explanation seems to be that empty nests and relative independence (financially and vocationally) can result in no longer getting what one or the other wants to *get* out of the marriage and looking to *get* from another lover. That raises the question of the basis of those marriages in the first place—likely not based on covenant and commitment to giving more than getting.

This then is the door of challenge and opportunity open to you in your life together. As you go forth as a team, remember God is able to do more than we know how to ask or think, and that for the glory of Christ who is Lord.

Prayer of Blessing (after the Exchange of Vows and Rings)

God, our Father in heaven, you have been witness to the covenant _____ and _____ have made—promising their faithfulness and love, and accepting the responsibilities of marriage. Be pleased to set your seal of blessing on this union for your glory and their fulfillment.

We praise you that even as you have led these to lives together you can enable theirs to be a happy, harmonious marriage. Bless this husband in his new role. Enable him to be strong, tender, and understanding. Bless this wife in her new relationship. Give her strength, patience, and a peace that comes from within.

As we celebrate their love and your faithfulness, we pray that you will help _____ and _____ to trust in you daily for the grace and wisdom to cope with life with its problems and necessary adjustments, and to do so in the strength of your Spirit.

I ask that you will give them eyes to see and sense your presence in all the circumstances of life that come to them. I pray that they may hear your voice of direction and encouragement. May both the good times and the bad times they experience serve to strengthen the bond of love between them and their appreciation of you, Lord.

Cause these precious moments of joy today to abide. Thank you that it is your intent for the marriage relationship to grow and become increasingly better with the years. Enable this couple to grow even closer in their journey together.

Bless the home they establish, so that it may be a testimony of your grace and love. And with any children you may give them, may they demonstrate in a confused world the fullness and joy of marriage in the Lord and a family that honors you. Make their lives fruitful as they serve you, and keep them together in love and trust until the moment of death separates them, or until Jesus comes.

For your presence with us today, we thank you. Stir up every marriage here with the power of your redeeming love, so that your holy intentions may be fulfilled in all our marriages.

Lord, we trust you for these blessings and praise you as we commit our lives and marriages to you. Bless the joyous hours that follow as family and friends mingle in fellowship. In the name of your Son Jesus we pray. Amen

Benediction

Now may the Creator-Redeemer God of love bestow on _____ and _____, and each one here, grace and peace for today and for each new day, so that the presence and power of the Spirit of Jesus shapes our lives to the glory of Jesus Christ, the Lord. Amen.

Appendix

VOCABULARY LISTS. Hebrew and Greek words; transliterations; basic grammatical forms (without noting tense or case); limited definitions and meanings; references (illustrative only); LXX translation { }, without transliterations.

HEBREW VOCABULARY

אָב (*ab*) n. m., father, ancestor [Gen 2:24] {LXX, πατήρ}

אַבָּא (*abba*) Aramaic, intense form of אָב n. m. father, "daddy"

אָדָם (*adam*) n. m., man, humankind, Adam [Gen 1:26; 4:25] {LXX, ἄνθρωπος, Αδάμ}

אָהַב (*ahab*) vb., love [Deut 6:5; 1 Sam 1:5; Hos 3:1] {LXX, ἀγαπάω (with few exceptions)}

אַהַב (*ahab*) n. m., love [Judg 16:4; Prov 5:19; 7:18; Hos 8:9] {LXX, ἀγάπη, φίλια, ἔρως}

אִישׁ (*ish*) n. m., man, husband, male, mate [Gen 2:24; 3:6, 16; 7] {LXX, ἄνθτωπος, ἀνήρ, ἄρσην}

אֵם (*em*) n. f., mother [Gen 2:24; 3:20] {LXX, μήτηρ}

אֱנוֹשׁ (*enosh*) n. m., man, human being, husband [Ps 8:4; Ruth 1:11] {LXX, ἄνθρωπος, ἀνήρ}

אָרַשׂ (*aras*) vb., betroth, become engaged, take as wife [Deut 22:23; Hos 2:19–20] {LXX, μνηστεύω}

אִשָּׁה (*ishah*) n. f., woman, wife [Gen 2:22–25; 11:29; 24:5–8] {LXX, γυνή}

בַּיִת־אָב (*bayit ab*), n. m., father's house(hold), paternal family [Gen 24:38; Num 30:16] {LXX, οἶκος πατρός}

בּוֹא (*bo*) vb., enter, go in to, cohabit with [Gen 16:2; Deut 22:13] {LXX , εἰσέρχομαι, συνοικέω}

בָּעַל (*baal*) vb., take possession of, marry a wife, get a husband [Gen 20:3; Deut 24:1] {LXX, λαμβάνω}

בַּעַל (*baal*) n. m., owner, master, husband [Prov 31:11, 23, 28] {LXX, ἀνήρ}

בְּרִית (*brit*) n. f., covenant [Mal 2:10, 14] {LXX, διαθήκη}

בָּשָׂר אֶחָד (*basar*) n. m., flesh; (*ekhad*) adj., one [Gen 2:24] {LXX, μία σάρξ}

גָּאַל (*gaal*) vb., redeem, do part of kinsman (for a woman, marry) [Ruth 3:13] {LXX, ἀγχιστεύω}

גֶּבֶר (*geber*) n. m., man, as distinct from woman, אִשָּׁה(*ishah*), or maid, עַלְמָה (*almah*) [Deut 22:5; Prov 30:19] {LXX, ἀνήρ}

גָּרַשׁ (*garash*) vb., cast out, divorce [Lev 21:7; Num 30:9] {LXX, ἐκβάλλω}

דָּבַק (*dabaq*) vb., cleave (sometimes with " or -), be attracted to, be devoted to [Gen 2:24; Gen 34:3; 1 Kgs 11:1–2] {LXX, προσκολλάω}

דּוֹד (*dod*) n. m., beloved one [Song 1:14] {LXX, ἀδελφιδός}

דְּמוּת (*dmut*) n. f., likeness [Gen 1:26; 5:1, 3] {LXX,ὁμοίωσις}

הָלַל (*halal*) vb., praise, celebrate, have a wedding song [Ps 78:63]

הָרָה (*harah*) vb., conceive, become/be pregnant [Gen 4:1;19:36; 2 Sam 11:5] {LXX, ἐν γαστρὶ λαμβάνειν}

זָכָר (*zakar*) n. m., male [Gen 1:27; 5:2; Lev 18:22] {LXX, ἄρσην}

זֹנָה (*zonah*) n. f., prostitute, harlot (common) [Gen 38:15; Josh 2:1; Isa 1:21] {LXX, πόρνη}

זְנוּת (*znut*) n. f., fornication, harlotry, unfaithfulness (to God, spouse) [Ezek 23:27] {LXX, πορνεία}

חֲבֶרֶת (*khaberet*) n. f., companion, partner [only in Mal 2:14] {LXX, κοινωνός}

חָבַר (*khabar*) vb., unite, be closely joined, tied together [Ps 122:3; Hos 4:17] {LXX, μετοχή}

חָם (*kham*) n. m., father-in-law [Gen 38:13, 25] {LXX, πενθερός}

חָמוֹת (*khamot*) n. f., mother-in-law [Ruth 1:14; 3:1] {LXX, πενθερά}

חָגַד (*khagad*) vb., desire strongly, covet [Exod 20:17; Prov 6:25] {LXX, ἐπιθυμέω}

חָשַׁק (*khashaq*) vb., love, attracted to [Deut 21:11] {LXX, ἐθυμέομαι}

חָתָן (*khatan*) n. m., daughter's husband, bridegroom, son-in-law [1 Sam 18:23; Isa 61:10] {LXX, γαμβρός, νυμφιός}

חָתַן (*khatan*) vb., marry, give in marriage, intermarry [Josh 23:12; Deut 7:3] {LXX, γαμβρεύω, ἐπιγραμβρεύω}

יָבָם (*yabam*) n., brother-in-law, husband's brother (levirate duty) [Deut 25:5]

יָבַם (*yabam*) vb., marry brother's wife (levirate) [Gen 38:8; Deut 25:7] {LXX , no specific parallel word}

יָדִיד (*yadid*) n. m., beloved [Deut 33:12] {LXX, form of ἀγαπάω}

יָדַע (*yada*) vb., know (also, sexual intercourse) [Gen 4:1; 1 Sam 1:19] {LXX, γινώσκω}

יָלַד (*yalad*) vb., give birth, to beget (father) [Gen 3:16; 11:27] {LXX, τίκτω, γεννάω}

יָשַׁב (*yashab*) vb., dwell, give dwelling (marry) [Ezra 10:17–18; Neh 13:23] {LXX, καθίζω}

כַּלָּה (*kallah*) n. f., daughter-in-law, bride, spouse [Ruth 1:6; Jer 2:32; Hos 4:13–14] {LXX, νυμφή}

כְּרִיתוּת (*kritut*) n. f., dismissal, divorcement (bill of) [Deut 24:1; Jer 3:8] {LXX, ἀποστάσιον}

כָּרַת (*karat*) vb., cut (as covenant); cut off (verb behind noun *kritut*)

לָקַח (*laqakh*) vb., obtain a wife, take (in marriage) [Gen 25:20; Ruth 4:13] {LXX, λαμβάνω}

מֹהַר (*mohar*) n. m., dowry, gift to bride's parents [Gen 34:12; Exod 22:17] {LXX, φερνή}

מִשְׁפָּחָה (*mishppakhah*) n. f., family, clan, tribe [Gen 12:3; 24:40] {LXX, N280}

נָאַף (*naap*) vb., commit adultery [Exod 20:14; Prov 30:20] {LXX, μοιχέω}

נִאֻף (*niup*) n. m., adultery (only in plural, נִאֻפִים) [Jer 13:27; Ezek 23:43] {LXX, μοιχεία}

נֶגֶד (*neged*) n. m., corresponding to [Gen 2:18, 20] {LXX has only prep. κατά}

נְקֵבָה (*nqebah*) (from נָקַב, pierce) n. f., female [Gen 5:2; Lev 12:5–7] {LXX, θῆλυς}

נָשָׂא (*nasa*) vb., carry, take on a wife, marry [Judg 21:23; Ezra 10:14] {LXX, λαμβάνω}

נָשִׁים (*nashim*) n. f. pl., women, wives (multiple) [Gen 18:11; Deut 17:17] {LXX, γυναῖκες}

עָגַב (*agab*) vb., lust, desire (sexual) [Ezek 23:7-12] {LXX, ἐπιτίθημι (Matt 5:28)}

עוֹנָה (*onah*) n. f., sexual intercourse, (?) lodging/shelter [Exod 21:10] {LXX, ὁμιλία}

עוּן (*un*) possible root (to dwell) for עוֹנָה

עָזַב (*azab*) vb., leave, let go, abandon [Gen 2:24] {LXX, καταλείπω}

עֵזֶר (*azer*) n. m., help, helper [Gen 2:18; Ps 33:20] {LXX, βοηθός}

עָזַר (*azar*) vb., help, enable [Ps 37:40] {LXX, βοηθέω}

עַלְמָה (*alma*) n. f., maiden, young woman, marriageable girl [Prov 30:19; Isa 7:14] {LXX, νεότης, παρθένος}

עֶצֶם (*etsem*) n. f., bone [Gen 2:23] {LXX, ὀστέον}

פִּלֶגֶשׁ (*pilegesh*) n. f., concubine [2 Sam 3:7; 5:13] {LXX, παλλακή}

צֶלֶם (*tselem*) n. m., image [Gen 1:26–27] {LXX, εἰκών}

קָדַשׁ (*qadash*) vb., consecrate [Exod 13:2] {LXX, ἁγιάζω}

קָדוֹשׁ (*qadosh*) adj., sacred, holy [Exod 19:6] {LXX, ἅγιος}

קָדֵשׁ (*qadesh*) n. m., male prostitute (cultic) [Deut 23:17–18; 2 Kgs 23:7] {LXX, no specific equivalent}

קְדֵשָׁה (*qdeshah*) n. f., female prostitute (cultic) [Deut 23:17] {LXX, πόρνη}

רֵעַ (*rea*) n. m., companion, husband [Jer 3:20] {LXX, ptc. σύνειμι}

שֵׁגָל (*shegal*) n. f., queen, consort [Neh 2:6; Dan 5:2] {LXX, παλλακή}

שָׁגַל (*shegal*) vb., have sex with, ravish [Deut 28:30; Isa 13:16] {LXX, ἔχω}

שָׁכַב (*shakab*) vb., lie (with), have sexual intercourse [Gen 39:10, 14; Lev 20:11–13] {LXX, καθεύδω, κοιμάομαι}

שָׁלַח (*shalakh*) vb., send away, let go, divorce [Deut 22:29] {LXX, ἐξαποστέλλω}

GREEK VOCABULARY [LXX, SEPTUAGINT]

ἄγαμος (*agamos*) adj., unmarried (man or woman) [1 Cor 7: 8, 11, 32, 34]

ἀγαπάω (*agapaō*) vb., love [John 3:16; Eph 5:25]

ἀγάπη (*agapē*) n. f., love [John 13:35]

ἁγιάξω (*hagiazō*) vb., sanctify, make holy [1 Cor. 7:14; Eph 5:26]

ἀνήρ (*anēr*) n. m., man, husband [Luke 1:27; 1 Cor 7:2]

ἄνθρωπος (*anthrōpos*) n. m., human (generic) [Matt 4:4], occasionally as male human [1 Cor 7:1]

ἀπολύω (*apolyō*) vb., let loose, release (divorce) [Matt 1:19; 5:31]

ἁρμόζω, ἁρμόζομαι (*harmozō, harmozomai*) vb., to fit together in marriage, betroth [2 Cor 11:2]

ἄρσην (*arsēn*) adj., male [Matt 19:4; Gal 3:28]

ἀρσενοκότης (*arsenokoitēs*) (combining *arsēn* and *koitē*) [1 Cor 6:9; 1 Tim 1:10]

ἀσέλγεια (*aselgeia*) n.f. sexual excess, lack of self-constraint [Rom 13:13; Eph 4:19]

αὐθεντεῖν (*authentein*) infin. to have dominion over (to claim to be originator of) [1 Tim 2:12]

αὐθεντέω / αὐθέντης v. and n. forms (possibly in the sense of being the author of)

ἀφίημι (*aphiēmi*) vb., send away, release, let go (divorce) [1 Cor 7:11–13]

γαμέω (*gameō*) vb., marry (of a man and of a woman), to take as spouse [Luke 14:20; 1 Tim 4:3] γαμίζω, γαμίσκω (*gamizō, gamiskō*) vb., give in marriage [Mark 12:25]

γάμος (*gamos*) n. m., marriage, wedding event/celebration [John 2:1–2; Heb 13:4]

γινώσκω (*ginōskō*) vb., know (also sexual intercourse) [Matt 1:25; Luke 1:34]

γυνή (*gynē*) n. f., adult female, woman, wife [Matt 5:28; 5:31–32]

δέω (*deō*) vb., bind [1 Cor 7:27, 39]

διαθήκη (*diathēkē*) n. f., covenant [Heb 8:8–9] (not used of marriage in New Testament)

δουλόω (*douloō*) vb., enslave (pass., be enslaved/bound to) [1 Cor 7:15]

ἐγκράτεια (*enkrateia*) n. f., self-control, restraint of one's impulses [Gal 5:23]

εἰκών (*eikōn*) n. f., image, likeness [1 Cor 11:7; Col 3:10]

εἷς (*heis*) adj., μία (*mia*) adj., one [Matt 19:5; 1 Cor 6:16]

εἰσέρχομαι (*eiserchomai*) vb., go in to (may have sexual connotation) [LXX, Gen 16:2; Deut 21:13]

ἐκβάλλω (*ekballō*) vb., throw out (divorce) [used of divorce in LXX, Lev 21:7, 14]

ἑνῶσις (*henōsis*) n. f., oneness, unity (not in LXX or New Testament)

ἐξαποστέλλω (*exapostellō*) vb., put away (divorce) [LXX, Deut 24:3]

ἐξουσία (*exousia*) n. f., authority [1 Cor 11:10]

ἐξουσιάζω (*exousiazō*) vb., have authority over [1 Cor 7:4]

ἐπιγαμβρεύω (*epigambreuō*) vb., marry (levirate provision) [LXX, Deut 25:5; Matt 22:24]

ἐπιθυμέω (*epithymeō*) vb., desire, covet, have sexual interest in [Matt 5:28]

ἐπιθυμία (*epithymia*) n. f., desire, passion [1 Thess 4:3-5]

ἐπιτίθημι (*epitithēmi*) vb., lay upon [LXX, Ezek 23:7–12 lust, dote on]

ἔρως (*erōs*) n. m., love (erotic) [not in New Testament, LXX, Prov 7:18] θῆλυς (*thēlys*) adj., female [Matt 19:4; Gal 3:28]

καταλείπω (*kataleipō*) vb., leave [Gen 2:24; Eph 5:31]

κεφαλή (*kephalē*) n. f., head [1 Cor 11:3–4]

κοιμάω, κοιμάομαι (*koimaō, koimomai*) vb., fall asleep, die [John 11:12] [LXX, Gen 47:30; also lay with (sexually) Gen 30:16; 2 Sam 11:4]

κοινωνός (*koinōnos*) n. m., partner, companion [LXX, Mal 2:14]

κοίτη (*koitē*) n. m., bed, marriage-bed [Heb 13:4]

κολλάω (*kollaō*) vb., join, cleave to, (lit. glue) [1Cor 6:16–17]

κύριος (*kyrios*) n. m. lord, sometimes for husband [1 Pet 3:6)] [LXX, Gen 18:12; and also the LXX rendering of) יהוה Yahweh]

μάλακος (*malakos*) n. m., soft, sexually passive [1 Cor 6:9]

μήτηρ (*mētēr*) n. f., mother [Prov 1:8; Matt 15:4]

μνηστεύω (*mnēsteuō*) vb., become engaged, to betroth [Matt 1:18]

μοιχεία (*moicheia*) n. f., adultery [Matt 15:19]

μοιχεύω (*moicheuō*) vb., commit adultery [Matt 5:27–28] [LXX, Exod 20:13]

νύμφη (*nymphē*) n. f., daughter-in-law, bride [LXX, Ruth 1:6; Matt 10:35; Rev 21:9]

νυμφίος (*nymphios*) n. m., bridegroom [Matt 25:1; John 2:9]

ὁμιλία (*homilia*) n .f., conversation, intercourse [LXX, Exod 21:10]

ὅμοιος (*homoios*) adj., like to, of same nature [LXX, Gen 2:20]

ὁμοίωσις (*homoiōsis*) n. f., likeness, resemblance [LXX, Gen 1:26; Jas 3:9]

πάθος (*pathos*) n. n., passion [1 Thess 4:5]

πατήρ (*patēr*) n. m., father [Eph 6:4]

πατριά (*patria*) n. f., family, clan [Acts 3:25; Eph 3:15]

πορνεία (*porneia*) n. f., prostitution, fornication [1Cor 6:18]

πόρνη (*pornē*) n. f., prostitute [1 Cor 6:15]

πόρνος (*pornos*) n. m., fornicator [Heb 13:4]

προσκολλάω (*proskollaō*) vb., join together, adhere to [Eph 5:31] [LXX, Gen 2:24]

σάρξ (*sarx*) n. f., flesh [Matt 19:5–6]

συζεύγνυμι (*syzeunymi*) vb., join together [Mark 10:5]

σύνειμι (*syneimi*) vb., be with. [LXX, Prov 5:19; no marital connotation in New Testament]

συνοικίζω (*synoikizō*) vb., dwell with, cohabit [LXX, Deut 21:13]

σῶμα (*sōma*) n. neut., body [1 Cor 6:15–16; 7:4]

σωφροσυνή (*sōphrosynē*) n. m., sound mind, moderation [1 Tim 2:9, 15]

τεκνογονία (*teknogonia*) n. f. childbearing [1 Tim 2:15]

ὕπανδρος (*hypandros*) adj., married, under a man [Rom 7:2]

ὑποτάσσω (*hypotassō*) vb., submit, to be subject to [Eph 5:21–24]

φιλία (*philia*) n. f., love (familial)

φοβέομαι (*phobeomai*) vb., φόβος (*phobos*) n. m., fear, respect [Eph 5:21, 33]

χωρίζω (*chōrizō*) vb., separate [Matt 19:6; 1 Cor 7:10]

NOTES ON MARRIAGE VOCABULARY

The vocabulary survey has included Hebrew and Greek words clustered around marriage. (These included both nouns and verbs, because corresponding verbs often shed light on the meaning of nouns.) Highlights of the findings are appended here for readers with interest in and at least some acquaintance with Hebrew and Greek. The differences and similarities pertaining to these two languages reveal overtly and sometimes subtly the understandings of marriage in the cultures out of which they come. Word meanings do not always remain constant. Comparing vocabulary usage is a way to trace any relevant changes in understandings of the concepts conveyed by the words. It is also the case that words may have more than one meaning, leaving the translator/exegete to choose which meaning best fits a given context. (Transliterations included.)

Appendix

PERTINENT HEBREW (OLD TESTAMENT) VOCABULARY

The several Hebrew words for husband and for wife carry nuances of meaning.

- Besides אִישׁ (*ish*), another common word for man/mankind, אֱנוֹשׁ (*enosh*), is also used for a human husband, and by implication for God in Ezekiel 16:45 (in a chapter laying out the whoredom and adultery of the people of Jerusalem).

- An often-used word for husband (especially in the earlier part of the Old Testament) comes from the root verb בָּעַל (*baal*), to take possession of, to rule over, thus giving the general meaning of owner (with a wife as a possession). This is also the name of a Canaanite god, Baal. Apart from association with idolatrous worship of Baal, the word did not have negative connotations. The husband of the praised woman in Proverbs 31:10–31 is בַּעַל. This Hebrew word is rendered as ἀνήρ (*anēr*) and ἀνδρός (*andros*) in LXX. The word designates Yahweh a number of times (e.g., Isa 54:5; Jer 3:14). The prediction in Hosea 2:16 that in the future when Yahweh takes his people as a wife they will call him "My husband" instead of "My Baal" likely has more to do with abandoning pagan idolatry than with redefining the marital relationship of God and people.

- Yet another word translated husband surfaces in the marriage analogy of Yahweh and Israel. Usually translated neighbor/friend/companion, in Jeremiah 3:20, as a faithless wife leaves her companion (husband) רֵעַ (*rea*), so Israel leaves Yahweh.

- A term used for husband חָתָן (*khatan*) in Exodus 4:25–26 and for bridegroom (and for father-in-law) stems from a root meaning to circumcise (*IDB*).[1] It reflects a custom of the bridegroom being circumcised by his father-in-law (a sign of inclusion in the Israelite family). The involvement of blood may have overtones of this being a covenant-ratifying sign. It's the term used for Jethro being the father-in-law of Moses. One form of the word is translated mother-in-law (Deut 27:23).

---

1. Baab, "Marriage," 285.

- The plural feminine noun נָשִׁים (*nashim*), although sometimes meaning simply women, is used frequently as wives in the sense of multiple wives of a husband.

- A word used several times for the king's wife (wives), שֵׁגַל (*shegal*), connotes what was associated with marriage out of the root שָׁגַל (*shagal*), meaning to lie with (also to violate, ravish). The noun form is used for queen and consort.

- Two words occur frequently for sexual intercourse: יָדַע (*yada*), to know (also in ordinary sense of knowing), and שָׁכַב (*shakab*), meaning to lie down with (also in ordinary sense of lying down).

- In Malachi 2:14, the "wife of your youth" is called חֲבֶרֶת (*khaberet*), meaning companion or partner, which the LXX renders as κοινωνός (*koinōnos*).

- A wife of secondary rank is termed a concubine, פִּלֶגֶשׁ (*pileges*), a word perhaps influenced by the Greek term for young girl παλλακή /παλλακίς (*pallakē/pallakis*). Occurring mostly in Judges, Samuel, Kings, and Chronicles, it signifies more than mistress. It was mostly men of wealth who had concubines. The female servants of wives are not specifically termed concubines and were apparently not available to the man of the household except with the permission or directive of his wife/wives.

- From a root word for "reserved for" we have the term כַּלָּה (*kallah*), which is imprecise regarding the point of marriage, translated as bride, young wife, spouse, and daughter-in-law. It is used in reference to Yahweh's bride (Isa 62:5; Jer 2:2).

A variety of words that are sometimes translated as marry/marriage convey elements of practices and understandings regarding marriage in the Old Testament.

- The verb לָקַח (*laqakh*), with a widely used meaning of take/receive/ acquire, is used of taking a wife (either for oneself or for a son or another person). It carries the connotation of acquiring a possession.

- The verb יָשַׁב (*yashab*) is widely used in the sense of dwell/remain/sit. Occurring only in Ezra 10 and Nehemiah 13, it means marry (in the sense of giving dwelling to, cohabiting).

- The verb נָשָׂא (*nasa*), used extensively as lift/carry/bear, occasionally has the meaning marry in the sense of taking on the responsibilities of a wife (also in Ezra and Neh).

- The verb יָבַם (*yabam*) reflects the levirate practice of performing the duty of a brother-in-law, that is, marry the widow and produce children (so the deceased would have descendants, Deut 25:5–10). Leviticus 18:16 and 20:21 prohibit a man marrying or having sexual relations with his brother's wife, without mentioning the exception of the levirate provision.

- The verb גָּאַל (*gaal*) for redeem also includes the levirate provision in Ruth 4, as the kinsman Boaz gets Ruth as wife as part of the re-demption of the property of Naomi (Ruth being the widow of one of Naomi's deceased sons).

- The verb חָתַן (*khathan*), from which the masculine noun rendered bridegroom comes (above), is used to indicate intermarriage with those of neighboring nations, including the sense of marriage alli-ances (Deut. 7:3; Josh 23:12; Ezra 9:14). A feminine noun form carries the meaning of marriage or wedding in Song of Songs 3:11.

- In Psalm 78:63, a word that is used extensively for praise (of God and humans), הָלַל (*halal*), is connected to marriage, with the sense that celebration (song) was part of the marriage event.

- The most common word translated father-in-law is חָם (*kham*). The feminine form, חָמוֹת (*khamot*), is then, as expected, mother-in-law.

- Two verbs carry the meaning of becoming engaged/espoused/be-trothed: אָרַשׂ (*aras*) and יָעַד (*yaad*), with a covenant price. Engagement was a time of preparation for marriage, not testing, as in our culture. The respective families are in agreement. It is almost as binding as marriage. The couple is committed exclusively, but do not cohabit or have sex. This practice had the value of assuring that the woman would not enter marriage pregnant by another man. If a man violated an engaged woman, it was considered adultery, the seducer was to be punished by death, and if she consented, the woman also (Deut 22:23–29). In Hosea 2:19–20, אָרַשׂ is used of Yahweh's engagement to Israel. Though short of marriage, it certainly includes intent and commitment to follow through.

- The Covenant Code (Exod 22:16–17) specifies that a seducer of a virgin, not engaged, must pay the "bride-price," מֹהַר (*mohar*), and marry the woman, but only if the father of the woman consents to the marriage. The price was not a purchase, in the sense of ownership, but part of the social agreement.

The terms father and mother and family are also included in the vocabulary review.

- The basic word for father is אָב (*ab*), apparently derived from an infant's first sounds directed to its father. (The noun occurs 1,191 times in the Hebrew Old Testament, plus 9 times more in Aramaic, אַבָּא [*abba*].) Usage is broader than the immediate male progenitor, sometimes used for grandfather, or more remote ancestor. The name Abram/Abraham is built on this basic term. It is also used of God, primarily metaphorically.

- The words for mother are אֲבִי (*abi*), counterpart of אָב, and אֵם (*em*), almost exclusively as female parent.

- Family is frequently a translation of מִשְׁפָּחָה (*mishpakhah*), often broader than nuclear family, with a meaning of clan, tribe, or nation. Often this noun is plural, and when singular or plural, it does not express relational aspects of family life. The sense of family is also often expressed as the father's house or household, בַּיִת־אָב (*bayit ab*), with patriarchal overtones.

- The word for conception as a result of sexual intercourse is generally הָרָה (*harah*), a word that can also carry the meaning of being with child and of bearing a child. Giving birth is a basic meaning of יָלַד (*yalad*), but is also the word translated beget, with reference to the male involvement in having children.

- The expression "one flesh" in Genesis 2:24 is בָּשָׂר אֶחָד (*basar ekhad*). The combination of "flesh" (one of the ways of designating the totality of being a person) with the much-used word for "one" connotes a unity that is more than physical union. (See comments on the Greek wording μία σάρξ (*mia sarx*) under the Greek New Testament vocabulary.)

Appendix

SEVERAL GREEK WORDS FROM THE LXX

The LXX rendering of Hebrew words associated with marriage provides us with how these concepts were being understood in the second century BC. New Testament usage of these Greek words then sheds light on the history of meanings.

The Hebrew vocabulary list includes the equivalent Greek words, except for a few cases in which the translation is idiomatic and does not include an equivalent word. The Greek vocabulary list includes some words used in LXX that are not in the New Testament vocabulary, but for which the lexicons provide evidence of meaning.

- Although the name of the Canaanite god Baal, בַּעַל, is transliterated as *Baal*, and retained in proper names incorporating these letters, the Greek form βααλ is not used for husband as in Hebrew (with the overtones of lord/master/ruler), rather usually using ἀνήρ (*anēr*) and ἀνδρός (*andros*), the most common words for man/husband, but sometimes κύριος (*kyrios*), meaning master/lord.

- A word with the literal meaning "under a man/husband," ὕπανδρος, (*hypandros*) modifying γυνή (*gynē*), the common word for woman or wife, designates a married woman (in Num 5:20, 29; Prov 6:24, 29).

- In Hosea 2:19–20 (2:21–22 in LXX) μνηστεύω (*mnēsteuō*) is translated as Yahweh saying he will take as a wife (NRSV), betroth (NIV), espouse (NAB) his people. BDAG adds "woo and win" to the meaning of the metaphor of becoming engaged, implying voluntary response and an emotional exchange. In several instances the verb translates אָרַשׂ (*aras*), the Hebrew word for betroth (as in Deut 20:7; 22:23) as the promise to move into human marriage. (Matthew and Luke use this Greek word for Mary's engagement to Joseph.)

- The word group γαμέω (*gameō*), γάμος (*gamos*), meaning marry/marriage, is rare in LXX (verb forms, γαμίζω, γαμίσκω, not found at all), although it appears in Tobit, 2 Maccabees, and 4 Maccabees, and in the New Testament. LXX follows the Hebrew pattern of saying daughters are given as wives, or to husbands (rather than in marriage, as interpreted in some English translations)

- In Jeremiah 3:20, LXX renders the Hebrew term רֵעַ (*rea*) with the Greek equivalent σύνειμι (*syneimi*), meaning the one being with her, as indicating husband. This Greek term is found also in Proverbs 5:19

in the marital relationship as: let her be with you at all times. The term is not used in this sense in the New Testament.

- A word used a few times for marry, ἐπιγαμβρεύω (*epigambreuō*) (also without the prefix), sometimes has the meaning of becoming one's father-in-law or son-in-law, and is sometimes translated intermarry. It also serves as the equivalent of) יָבַם *yabam*), meaning to marry the widow of a brother who has died childless (Gen 38:8). However, the levirate provision in Deuteronomy 25:5–10 (LXX) does not make use of this word.

- LXX continues the Hebrew pattern of expressing sexual intercourse as "know." The Hebrew יָדַע (*yada*) becomes γινώσκω (*ginōskō*) in Greek, from Genesis 4:1 on. (It is found once in the New Testament in this sense, in Matt 1:25.)

- In Proverbs 19:14, the verb ἁρμόζω (*harmozō*) is used to say that the Lord suits a wife to a husband. Elsewhere this verb had the sense of harmonizing, tuning an instrument, thus suggesting the musical metaphor of consonance in marriage.

- The words κοιμάομαι (*koimaomai*) (lie with, be abed, sleep, die) and κοίτη (*koitē*) (bed, nest, act of going to bed, marriage-bed) both also refer to sexual activity. Greek usage is parallel to the English expression "sleeping with," most frequently in an illicit relationship. From κοίτη we get the word coitus.

- The terms νύμφη (*nymphē*) (fem.) and νυμφίος (*nymphios*) (masc.) carry the sense of daughter-in-law and son-in-law (respectively) as well as bride and bridegroom. The feminine form is not precise as to marital status, ranging from young woman of marriageable age to espoused to be married to newly married to young wife. That broad range begs for translation decisions in Song of Solomon, where the term appears alongside sister. (The Brenton English translation of LXX opts for "spouse" in those texts.) Along with the human family relationships, these terms picture the people as bride, and the Lord, κύριος (*kyrios*), as bridegroom (Isa 62:5; Jer 2:32).

- A common word for a family unit is πατρία (*patria*), standing as the equivalent of both מִשְׁפָּחָה (*mishpakhah*) and בַּיִת־אָב (*bayit ab*). It identifies units with a common progenitor, often in the sense of people, clan, or tribe. Πατρία, derived from πατήρ (*patēr*, father), has the sense of the father's family tree. But it is not used in the sense of "fatherhood" as an abstract concept.

- A verb for conceiving is συλλαμβάνω (*syllambanō*), used twenty-four times in LXX for הָרָה (*harah*) in the sense of to become or be pregnant. (In the New Testament it occurs only several times, in Luke's pre-birth narratives.)

- Two verbs, γεννάω (*gennaō*) and τίκτω (*tiktō*) are used in the LXX (and New Testament) for "begetting" by the father and "bearing" by the mother.

- The LXX uses ἐκβάλλω (*ekballō*) and ἐξαποστέλλω (*exapostellō*) to express the putting away of divorce. The New Testament does not use these verbs for divorce, but rather ἀπολύω (*apolyō*) and ἀφίημι (*aphiēmi*).

PERTINENT GREEK (NEW TESTAMENT) VOCABULARY

- The Greek word for male human being is ἀνήρ (*anēr*) and is the primary word for both man and husband. The generic term for human being, ἄνθρωπος (*anthrōpos*), is misleadingly translated as "man" in most versions. Several cotemporary translations go with plural pronouns and "human beings," or "mortals," to avoid the masculine limitation of "man."

- The Greek word for female human being (adult assumed) is γυνή (*gynē*), and is the primary word for both woman and wife.

- The New Testament also uses two gender specific terms: ἄρσην (*arsēn*) for male, and θῆλυς (*thēlys*) for female.

- Terms for bride, νύμφη (*nymphē*), and bridegroom, νυμφίος (*nymphios*), have meanings parallel with their Hebrew equivalents. However, whereas in the Old Testament Yahweh is bridegroom and Israel is bride, Jesus used bridegroom in a messianic sense fourteen times. Several parables are noteworthy. Matthew 9:15 implies that the wedding festivities have already begun. Matthew 25:1–13 focuses on activities when Christ/the bridegroom returns. Interestingly, the bride is not identified in Jesus's parable, the focus being on the readiness of the guests. Revelation 21:9 equates the bride, νύμφη (*nymphē*), with the wife, γυνή (*gynē*), of the Lamb, revealed as the Holy City (the redeemed people of God).[2]

- We find two words for betrothal, μνηστεύω (*mnēsteuō*) of Mary's engagement to Joseph, and ἁρμόζω (*harmozō*) in 2 Corinthians 11:2 where Paul writes "I promised you in marriage to one husband, to present you as a chaste virgin to Christ." As with the terms bride and bridegroom noted above, this text envisions the church, the saints, as the bride-to-be of Christ. Outside the New Testament both words are used of human espousal.

- A verb, ἐπικαλέω (*epikaleō*), has the meaning of naming/calling on. As a passive it has the sense of taking the name of or receiving the name of, sometimes translated "surnamed." It carries the connotation of belonging to. William Barclay notes that this word is used of a wife taking the name of her husband in marriage, and of a child being called by his father. In comments on James 2:7 he says: "The Christian takes the name of Christ; he is called after Christ. It is as if he was married to Christ, or born and christened into the family of Christ."[3] This then is another example of the relationship of Christ and a believer expressed in the imagery of betrothal and marriage.

- The verb γαμέω (*gameō*), marry, is used of both men and women in 1 Corinthians 7 (and possibly implied in 1 Tim 4:3). The variations γαμίζω (*gamizō*) and γαμίσκω (*gamiskō*) both mean give in marriage. Jesus's teaching in Matthew 24:38 and in Mark 12:25 (par. Luke 20:34) reflects the traditional culture—men marrying and women being given in marriage.

- Marriage as a noun, γάμος (*gamos*), refers almost always to a wedding and the associated celebration, rather than to the ongoing relationship or the institution of marriage. Extended celebrations are reflected in Luke 12:36 and John 2:1–11. However, in one text, Hebrews 13:4, marriage as continuing marital status is affirmed as honorable. Here, marriage is viewed positively, compared with 1 Timothy 4:3, in which false teachers forbade marriage and other things God has created good.

2. For an extensive discussion of Christ as bridegroom, see Jeremias, "νύμφη, νυμφίος," 1099–106.

3. Barclay, *The Letters of James and Peter*, Daily Study Bible Series, 67.

- One word for bed, κοίτη (*koitē*), also means marriage-bed (and the assumed sexual activity) in Hebrews 13:4, with the admonition that it not be defiled by marital unfaithfulness. This word, from which the English word coitus comes, carries a veiled reference to sexual intercourse and the way children are conceived (Rom 9:10), and is used of sexual excess (Rom 13:13).

- Matthew 19:6 (par. Mark 10:9) has Jesus using συζεύγνυμι (*syzeunnumi*) to say what God does in marriage—joining the couple together. The word in non-biblical usage means yoke/join together. It thus conveys a sense of being matched in a team. In Ezekiel 1 (LXX) it is used of a pair of wings. (It takes two to fly!)

- The question to Jesus about marriage in Matthew 22:24 contains the word ἐπιγαμβρεύω (*epigambreuō*), alluding to the levirate provision and practice.

- In Romans 7:2 (and only there in the New Testament) a married woman is identified as under a man/husband, ὕπανδρος (*hupandros*), a term found several times in LXX with the same implied understanding of marriage.

- A word for unmarried, ἄγαμος (*hagamos*), surfaces in 1 Corinthians 7, a marital status not recognized in the Old Testament (LXX). It appears once in the Apocrypha (LXX, 4 Macc 16:9).

- A deliberate emphasis on "one," εἷς (*heis*) (masc.) and μία (*mia*) (fem.), stands out in reference to marital relations: one flesh; two become one; promised to one husband; husband of one wife. Singular marital unity seems to be connected to the theological understanding of God as one.

- The expression "one flesh," μία σάρξ (*mia sarx*), in Matthew 19:5, 6; Mark 10:8; and Ephesians 5:31 clearly refers to Genesis 2:24. The same expression in 1 Corinthians 6:16 is about union with a prostitute. The word "henosis," ἑνῶσις, also meaning oneness/unity, not used in the New Testament, is from the same word family. It is found in Ignatius to Polycarp 5:2, meaning marriage. The term was also used extensively in the debates of the post-apostolic church about the person of Christ. The term "henosis," as applied to marriage, can help to express the ontological aspect of sexual union. The oneness conveyed by these several words and expressions entails much more than physical intercourse.

- The extensively used term for father in the Greek language is πατήρ (*patēr*). It was used in a religious sense (in Greek and Roman mythologies) as well as for identifying the male parent. The same term is then applied to God, especially through the usage and teachings of Jesus. The companion term for mother is μήτηρ (*mētēr*), used mostly as female parent, but also metaphorically as source.

Bibliography

Achtemeier, Elizabeth. *Nahum–Malachi.* Interpretation. Atlanta: John Knox, 1986.

Achtemeier, Paul J. *1 Peter.* Hermeneia. Minneapolis, MN: Fortress, 1996.

Ahituv, Shmuel. "Did God Really Have a Wife?" Review of *Did God Have a Wife?* William G. Dever, *Biblical Archeology Review.* Sept–Oct 2006, 62–66.

Alford, Henry. *The New Testament for English Readers.* Chicago: Moody, n.d.

Ali, Abdullah Yusuf, trans. *The Holy Quran.* New Delhi, India: Goodword, 2003.

Amstutz, H. Clair. *Marriage in Today's World.* Scottdale, PA: Herald, 1978.

Arndt, William F., and F. Wilbur Gingrich. *Greek-English Lexicon of the New Testament and other Early Christian Literature,* 4th ed. Chicago: University of Chicago, 1957.

Associated Press. "Census Records Big Increase in Unmarried Couples." *Salem News* (Salem, Ohio) May 15, 2001, 5A.

Baab, Otto J. "Marriage." *IDB 3,* 278–87.

Bailey, Derrick Sherwin. *The Mystery of Love and Marriage.* New York: Harper and Brothers, 1952.

Barclay, William. *The Daily Bible Study Series,* revised ed. Philadelphia, PA: Westminster, 1976.

Barnette, Henlee H. "Coarchy: Partnership and Equality in Man-Woman Relationships." *Review & Expositor,* LXXV/1 (1978), 19–24.

Barrett, C. K. *The First Epistle to the Corinthians.* Harper's New Testament Commentaries. New York: Harper & Row, 1968.

———. *The Second Epistle to the Corinthians.* Harper's New Testament Commentaries. New York: Harper & Row, 1973.

Barth, Karl. *Church Dogmatics, III.* Edinburgh, Scotland: T. & T. Clark, 1961.

Barth, Marcus. *Ephesians 4–6.* Anchor Bible. Garden City, NY: Doubleday, 1974.

Barton, Stephen C., ed. *The Family in Theological Perspective.* Edinburgh, Scotland: T. & T. Clark, 1996.

———. "Living as Families in the Light of the New Testament." *Interpretation,* 52/2 (1998) 130–44.

Batto, Bernard F. "The Institution of Marriage in Genesis 2 and Atrahasis." *Catholic Biblical Quarterly,* 62/4 (2000), 621–31.

Bauer, Walter, et al. *English Lexicon of the New Testament and Other Early Christian Literature, BDAG,* 3rd edition. Chicago: University of Chicago, 1971.

Beeston, A. F. L. "One Flesh." *Vetus Testamentum,* January 1986, 115–17.

Bell, Albert A. *A Guide to the New Testament World.* Scottdale, PA: Herald, 1994.

Bender, Harold S., and C. Henry Smith. *Mennonite Encyclopedia* (ME), Vols. 1–4. Scottdale, PA: Herald, 1955–59.

Bender, Ross T. *Christians in Families.* Scottdale, PA: Herald, 1982.

Bibliography

BibleWorks 8.0, Norfolk, VA, 2008. *BDAG*; *HALOT*; *Abridged Liddell-Scott Greek English Lexicon*; *Louw-Nida Greek-English Lexicon of the New Testament*, 1988; *Septuagintia* by Alfred Rahlfs; *Biblia Hebraica Stuttgartensia*; LXX in English (Brenton); *Nestle-Aland Greek New Testament (27th Edition)*; all the common English translations.

Bird, Phyllis A. "Male and Female He Created Them." *Harvard Theological Review*, 74 (1981) 129–59.

Bland, Thomas A. "Toward a Theology of Marriage." *Review & Expositor*, LXI/2 (1964) 6–13.

Blankenhorn, David, et al., eds. *Does Christianity Teach Male Headship?* Grand Rapids: Eerdmans, 2004.

Boettner, Loraine. *Roman Catholicism*. Chap. XV, "Marriage." Philadelphia, PA: Presbyterian and Reformed, 1962.

Botterweck, G. Johannes and Helmer Ringgren, eds. *Theological Dictionary of the Old Testament* (TDOT), 15 vols. Grand Rapids, MI: Eerdmans, 1974, 2003.

Bracher, Marjory Louise. *Love Is No Luxury*. Philadelphia, PA: Fortress, 1968.

Brenton, Lancelot Lee, trans. *Septuagint Version of the Old Testament*. London: Bagster, n.d.

Bromiley, Geoffrey W., ed. *Theological Dictionary of the New Testament* (TDNT), 10 Vols. Grand Rapids, MI: Eerdmans, 1964.

Brown, Francis, et al., eds. *Hebrew and English Lexicon of the Old Testament*. London: Oxford University, 1955.

Browning, Don S., et al. *From Culture Wars to Common Ground*. Grand Rapids, MI: Eerdmans, 1997.

————. *Marriage and Modernization: How Globalization Threatens Marriage and What to Do About It*. Grand Rapids, MI: Eerdmans, 2003.

————, et al. *Sex, Marriage and Families in World Religions*. New York: Columbian University, 2006.

————. "Putting Marriage on the Agenda Again." Interview by Thomas Knieps-Port le Roi, *INTAMS Review*, Vol 11/1 (2005).

Bruce, F. F. *1 & 2 Corinthians*. New Century Bible Commentary. Grand Rapids, MI: Eerdmans, 1971.

————. *Commentary on the Epistle to the Hebrews*. New London Commentary on the New Testament. Edinburgh, Scotland: Marshall, Morgan, and Scott, 1964.

Brueggemann, Walter. "Of the Same Flesh and Bone." *Catholic Biblical Quarterly*, 32, (1970).

Bushnell, Catherine. *God's Word to Women*. Jacksonville, FL: Ray B. Munson, 1923.

Buttrick, George A., ed. *Interpreter's Dictionary of the Bible, IDB*. Vols. 1–4. Nashville, TN: Abingdon, 1962. *IDB* Supplementary Volume, 1976.

Campbell, Ken M., ed. *Marriage and Family in the Biblical World*. Downers Grove, IL: Inter-Varsity, 2003.

Charen, Mona. "Few Babies to Adopt." *Salem News*, Salem, Ohio, 07-17-00.

Charles, Howard H. *Opening the Bible*. Chapter 10, "Sex, Marriage and the Bible." Institute of Mennonite Studies, Elkhart, IN and Herald, Scottdale, PA, 2005.

Cohen, Abraham. *Everyman's Talmud*. New York: E. P. Dutton, 1949.

Cohen, Shaye J., DA. *The Jewish Family in Antiquity*. Atlanta: Scholars, 1993.

Cole, William Graham. *Sex and Love in the Bible*. New York: Association, 1959.

Confession of Faith in a Mennonite Perspective. Scottdale, PA: Herald, 1995.

Bibliography

Coolidge, David Orgon. "The Dilemma of Same-Sex Marriage." *Crisis Online*, July/August 1996.

Dearman, J. Andrew. "The Family in the Old Testament." *Interpretation,* 52/2 (1998), 117–29.

———. "Marriage in the Old Testament." In *Biblical Ethics and Homosexuality: Listening to Scripture*, R. Brawley, ed., 53–67. Louisville, KY: Westminster/John Knox, 1996.

Deming, W. *Paul on Marriage and Celibacy: The Hellenistic Background of 1 Cor. 7.* Grand Rapids: Eerdmans, 2004.

Dobson, Dr. James. *Dare to Discipline.* Wheaton, IL: Tyndale House, 1992.

Donoghue, Susanne Coalson. *Meditaitons for Single Moms.* Scottdale, PA: Herald, 1997.

Dyck, Cornelius J., and Dennis D. Martin. *Mennonite Encyclopedia* (ME), Vol. 5. Scottdale, PA: Herald, 1990.

Edersheim, Alfed. *Sketches of Jewish Social Life in the Days of Christ.* Grand Rapids, MI: Eerdmans, 1980 (reprint).

Editors. *Christian Century.* "Divorce Culture," 11-01-2000.

Elias, Jacob W. *1 & 2 Thessalonians.* Believers Church Bible Commentary. Scottdale, PA: Herald, 1995.

Ellison, H. L. *Ezekiel, the Man and His Message.* London: The Paternoster, 1956.

Ewald, George R. *Jesus and Divorce.* Scottdale, PA: Herald, 1991.

Fee, Gordon D. *1 & 2 Timothy and Titus.* New International Biblical Commentary. Peabody, MA: Hendrickson, 1984.

Finger, Thomas N. *Christian Theology an Eschatological Approach*, Vol. II. Scottdale, PA: Herald, 1989.:

Freedman, David Noel, ed. *Anchor Bible Dictionary (ABD).* New York: Doubleday, 1992.

Gardner, Richard B. *Matthew.* Believers Church Bible Commentary. Scottdale, PA: Herald, 1991.

Geddert, Timothy J. *Mark.* Believers Church Bible Commentary. Scottdale, PA: Herald, 2001.

Girdlestone, Robert Baker. *Synonyms of the Old Testament.* Grand Rapids, MI: Eerdmans, 1948.

Gold, Rabbi Michael. "Traditional Sources on Sex outside Marriage." In *Does God Belong in the Bedroom.* Online: www.MyJewishLearning.com/.

Graetz, Naomi. "Domestic Violence in Jewish Law, How Judaism Views Wife-beating." Online: www.MyJewishLearning.com/.

Green, Joel B. "Scripture and Theology." *Interpretation,* 56/1 (2002) 5–20.

Grimsrud, Ted, and Mark Thiessen Nation. *Reasoning Together: A Conversation on Homosexuality.* Scotsdale, PA: Herald, 2008.

Guenther, Allen R. *Hosea, Amos.* Believers Church Bible Commentary. Scottdale, PA: Herald, 1998.

Harris, R. Laird, et al., eds. *Theological Wordbook of the Old Testament (TDOT).* Chicago: Moody, 1980.

Harrison, Everett F., ed. *Baker Dictionary of Theology.* Grand Rapids, MI: Baker, 1960.

Haught, Nancy. *Religious News Service, Mennonite Weekly Review.* Paul Schrag, ed. Newton, KS: March 12, 2007.

Henderson, Suzanne Watts. "Taking Liberties with the Text: The Colossian Household Code as Hermeneutical Paradigm." *Interpretation,* 60, 4 (2006) 420–32.

Hershberger, Anne Krabill. *Sexuality, God's Gift.* Scottdale, PA: Herald, 1999.

Bibliography

Hicks, Robert M. *The Christian Family in Changing Times*. Grand Rapids, MI: Baker, 2002.

Horowitz, Maryanne Cline, "The Image of God in Man—Is Woman Included?" *Harvard Theological Review*, 72, (1979).

Houghton, Kristen. "Divorce and Age," 2008. Online: www.familylobby.com/.

Hugenberger, Gordon P. *Marriage as a Covenant*. Grand Rapids, MI: Baker, 1994.

Instone-Brewer, David. "What God Has Joined, What Does the Bible Really Teach about Divorce?" *Christianity Today*, October 5, 2007, 26–29.

INTAMS, International Academy for Marital Spirituality. Brussels, Belgium. Online: www.intams.org/.

Janzen, Waldemar. *Exodus*. Believers Church Bible Commentary. Scottdale, PA: Herald, 2000.

Jeremias, Joachim. "νύμφη, νυμφίος. *TDNT 4*, 1099–106.

Jewett, Paul K. *Man as Male and Female*. Grand Rapids, MI: Eerdmans, 1975.

Jones, Serene. "Bounded Openness, Postmodernism, Feminism, and the Church Today." *Interpretation* 55/1 (2001) 49–59.

Kaufman, Gerald W. and L. Marlene. *Freedom Fences*. Scottdale, PA: Herald, 1999.

———. *Monday Marriage: Celebrating the Ordinary*. Scottdale, PA: Herald 2005.

———. "When friendships go too far." *The Mennonite*, Everett J. Thomas, ed. Goshen, IN: March 21, 2006, 11–13.

Keener, Craig S. *Paul, Women, and Wives: Marriage and Women's Ministry in the Letters of Paul*. Peabody, MA: Hendrickson, 1992.

Keil, C. F., and F. Delizsch. *Commentaries on the Old Testament, Pentateuch, Vol. 1*. Grand Rapids, MI: Eerdmans, 1951.

Kelly, J. N. D. *The Pastoral Epistles, Timothy 1 & 2, and Titus*. Harper's New Testament Commentaries. New York: Harper & Row, 1960.

Kerns, Joseph E., SJ. *The Theology of Marriage*. New York: Sheed and Ward, 1964.

Koehkler, Ludwig, et al. *Hebrew and Aramaic Lexicon of the Old Testament* (HALOT). Boston: Brill Academic, 1994.

Kohlenberger III, John R., ed. *NIV Interlinear Hebrew-English Old Testament*. Grand Rapids, MI: Zondervan, 1982.

Knight, David. *The Good News about Sex*. Cincinnati, OH: St. Anthony Messenger, 1979.

Kroeger, Richard Clark and Catherine Clark. *I Suffer Not a Woman*. Grand Rapids, MI: Baker, 1992.

Lake, Kirsopp, trans. *Apostolic Fathers*. 2 Vols. New York: Putnam's Sons, 1919.

Landy, Francis. "The Song of Songs and the Garden of Eden." *Journal of Biblical Literature*, 98 (1979) 513–28.

Lamm, Rabbi Maurice. "Explaining the *ketubah* (marriage contract) Text." In *The Jewish Way in Love and Marriage*, Jonathan David. Online: www.MyJewishLearning.com/.

Lederach, Paul M. *The Spiritual Family and the Biological Family*. Scottdale, PA: Herald, 1973.

Logan, Chantal. "Is the Gospel Good News for Muslim Women?" In *Anabaptists Meeting Muslims*. James R. Krabill, et al., eds., Scottdale, PA: Herald, 2005.

Marthaler, Bernard L., ed. *New Catholic Encyclopedia*, 2nd ed. Farmington Hills, MI: Thomson Gale, 2003.

Martin, Ernest D. *Colossians–Philemon*. Believers Church Bible Commentaries. Scottdale, PA: Herald, 1993.

McGee, P. Daniel. "The Inti-Mate Marriage." *Review & Expositor*, 98/1 (2001) 191–206.

McGlone, Lee. "Genesis 2:18–24; Ephesians 5:21—6:9." *Review & Expositor*, 86/2 (1989) 243–47.

Meeks, Wayne A. *The First Urban Christians*. New Haven, CT/London: Yale University, 1983.

————. "The Image of the Androgyne: Some Uses of Symbols in Earliest Christianity." *History of Religions*, 13 (1974) 165–208.

Mennonite Central Committee, Resources. "Home Shouldn't Be a Place that Hurts." Akron, PA. Online: www.mcc.org/.

Mennonite Church and General Conference Mennonite Church. *Human Sexuality in the Christian Life, A Working Document for Study and Dialogue*. Newton, KS: Faith and Life and Scottdale, PA: Mennonite, 1985.

Miller, John W. *Biblical Faith and Fathering*. New York: Paulist, 1989.

————. *Calling God Father, Essays on the Bible, Fatherhood and Culture*. New York: Paulist, 1999.

————. *Proverbs*. Believers Church Bible Commentary. Scottdale, PA: Herald, 2004.

Monsch-Rinderknecht, Christoph. *Unser JA–Impulse für eine lebendige Ehe (Four Marriage Enrichment Weekends for German-Speaking Couples in the Swiss Reformed Church)*. Liestalm Sweitz: Regoidruck, 2008.

Morrish, George. *Concordance of the Septuagint*. Grand Rapids, MI: Zondervan, 1976.

Neff, Christian. "Ban." *ME I*, 1995, 219–23.

Neufeld, Tom Yoder. *Ephesians*. Believers Church Bible Commentary. Scottdale, PA: Herald, 2002.

Oates, Wayne E. "The Church, Divorce, and Remarriage." *Review & Expositor*, LXI/2 (1964) 45–60.

Oden, Thomas C. *First and Second Timothy and Titus*. Interpretation. Louisville, KY: John Knox, 1989.

Oepke, Albecht. "γυνή," *TDNT 1*, 776–89.

Orr, James, ed. *International Standard Bible Encyclopedia*. Grand Rapids, MI: Eerdmans, 1946.

Osiek, Carolyn, and David L. Balch. *Families in the New Testament World*. Louisville, KY: Westminster John Knox, 1997.

————. "The Family in Early Christianity." *Catholic Biblical Quarterly*, 58 (1966) 1–25.

Parker, Simon B. "Marriage Blessing in Israelite/Ugartic Literature." *Journal of Biblical Literature*, 95 (1976) 23–30.

Patai, Raphael. *Sex and Family in the Bible*. Garden City, NY: Doubleday, 1959.

Perdue, Leo G., et al. *Families in Ancient Israel*. Louisville, KY: Westminster John Knox, 1997.

Piper, Otto A. *The Biblical View of Sex and Marriage*. New York: Charles Scribner's Sons, 1960.

Popenoe, David. "The Future of Marriage in America." The State of Our Unions, 2007, The National Marriage Project. Online: www.marriage.rutgers.edu/.

Quell, Gottfried. "ἀγαπάω." *TDNT 1*, 21–35.

Quinn, Jerome D. *Titus*. Anchor Bible. Garden City, NY: Doubleday, 1990.

Ramachandra, Vinoth. *Gods That Fail*. Downers Grove, IL: InterVarsity, 1996.

————. *The Recovery of Mission*. Grand Rapids, MI: Eerdmans, 1996.

Ringgren, H. "The Marriage Motif in Israelite Religion." In *Ancient Israelite Religion*, P. D. Miller et al., eds, 421–28. Philadelphia, PA: Fortress, 1987.

Robinson, Laurie Oswald (with Alfonso). "Many Waters Cannot Quench Love." *The Mennonite*. Everett J. Thomas, ed. Goshen, IN. March 21, 2006, 8–10.

Ropp, Eugene F. *Genesis*. Believers Church Bible Commentary. Scottdale, PA: Herald, 1987.

Sampley, J. Paul. "And the Two Shall Become One Flesh." *Society for New Testament Studies Monograph Series*, 16 (1971).

Schauss, Hayyim. "The Evolution of Marriage: Ancient." In *The Lifetime of a Jew Throughout the Ages of Jewish History*, UAHC, n. d. Online: www.MyJewishLearning.com/.

Schlier, Heinrich. "κεφαλή," *TDNT 3*, 673–81.

Schweizer, Eduard and Friedrich Baumgärtel. "σάρξ," *TDNT 7*, 98–151.

———. "σῶμα." *TDNT 7*, 1024–94.

Siddiqui, Shahina. "Marriage in Islam." Online: www.SoundVision.com/, 2006.

Sider, Ron J. *Doing Evangelism Jesus' Way: How Christians Demonstrate the Good News*. Nappanee, IN: Evangel, 2003.

Small, Dwight Hervey. *Christian: Celebrate Your Sexuality*. Old Tappan, NJ: Revell, 1974.

———. *Design for Christian Marriage*. Westwood, NJ: Revell, 1959.

Smedes, Lewis B. *Sex for Christians*. Grand Rapids: Eerdmans, 1976.

Smith, Ralph L. Micah–Malachi. Word Biblical Commentary. Waco, TX: Word, 1984.

Stagg, Evelyn and Frank. *Woman in the World of Jesus*. Philadelphia, PA: Westminster, 1978.

Stienstra, Nelly. *YHWH Is the Husband of His People*. Dampen: Kok Pharos, 1993.

Stowasser, Barbara Freyer. *Women in the Qur'an, Traditions, and Interpretation*. New York: Oxford University, 1994.

Swartley, Willard M. *Homosexuality, Biblical Interpretation, and Moral Discernment*. Scottdale, PA: Herald, 2003.

———. *Slavery, Sabbath, War, and Women*. Scottdale, PA: Herald, 1983.

Swidler, Arlene, ed. *Marriage in the World Religions, Journal of Ecumenical Studies*. XXII (1) 1985.

Thayer, Joseph Henry. *Greek-English Lexicon of the New Testament*. New York: American, 1889.

Thomas, Gary. *Sacred Marriage*. Grand Rapids, MI: Zondervan, 2000.

Toews, John E. "Women in Church Leadership." In *The Bible and the Church*, A. J. Dueck, et al., eds. Winnipeg, MB/Hillsboro, KS: Kindred, 1988.

Towner, H. Sibley. "Clones of God, Genesis 1:26–28, and the Image of God in the Hebrew Bible." *Interpretation*, 59/4 (2005).

Van Leeuwen, Mary Stewart. "Is Equal Regard in the Bible." In *Does Christianity Teach Male Headship*, Blankenhorn, et al., 13–22. Grand Rapids: Eerdmans, 2004.

Von Allmen, J.-J., ed. *Companion to the Bible*. New York: Oxford University, 1958.

Waltner, Erland. *1 Peter*. Believers Church Bible Commentary. Scottdale, PA: Herald, 1999.

Wenham, Gordon J. *Genesis I*. Word Biblical Commentary. Waco, TX: Word, 1987.

White, Ernest. *Marriage and the Bible*. Nashville: Broadman, 1965.

Whitehead, Barbara Dafoe, and Marline Pearson. "Making a Love Connection." Online: www.marriage.rutgers.edu/, 2007.

Whitehead, Barbara Dafoe. "Marriage—Just a Piece of Paper?" PBS Documentary, 2002.

Wigram, George V. *Englishman's Greek Concordance of the New Testament*, 9th ed. Grand Rapids, MI: Zondervan, 1970.

Bibliography

———. *Englishman's Hebrew and Chaldean Concordance of the Old Testament,* 5th ed. Grand Rapids, MI: Zondervan, 1970.

Winter, Bruce W. *Roman Wives, Roman Widows: The Appearance of New Women and the Pauline Communities.* Grand Rapids: Eerdmans, 2003.

Wright, Wendy M. "Spiritual Friendship between Men and Women." *International Christian Digest,* October 1988, 21–23.

Yamauchi, Edwin M. "Cultural Aspects of Marriage in the Ancient World." *Bibliotheca Sacra,* 135 (1979) 241–52.

Yarbrough, O. J. *Not Like the Gentiles: Marriage Rules in the Letters of Paul, Society of Biblical Literature Dissertation Series,* 80. Atlanta: Scholars, 1981.

Yeats, John R. *Revelation.* Believers Church Bible Commentary. Scottdale, PA: Herald, 2003.

Yoder, Bruce, and Imo Jeanne Yoder, eds. *Single Voices.* Scottdale, PA: Herald, 1982.

Yoder, John H. *The Politics of Jesus.* Grand Rapids, MI: Eerdmans, 1972.

Zehnder, Markus. "A Fresh Look at Malachi 2:12–16." *Vetus Testamentum,* 53/2, (2003) 224–59.

Zvi, Ehud Ben. "The Marital Metaphor of YHWH and Israel." *Journal for the Study of the Old Testament,* 28/3, (2004) 363–84.

Abbreviated Scripture Index

(some locations of pertinent texts)

OLD TESTAMENT

Genesis

1:26–28	18–20
1:27	23–25, 29, 80
2:18–25	21–23
2:23	22–23, 34–35
2:24	21–25, 29–30, 80, 142
3:16	73

Exodus

21:10–11	51–52

Deuteronomy

24:1–4	77–78
25:5–10	50, 141

Ezra

9–10	79

Proverbs

	58, 88
5:15–20	41
19:14	25, 144

Song of Solomon

	41–42

Hosea

1–3	79

Malachi

2:10–16	35–37, 49, 52

NEW TESTAMENT

Matthew

5:27–28	58, 98
5:31–32	79–82
12:46–50	60
19:3–9	23–24, 79–82

Mark

10:2–12	23–24, 79–81
10:11	58

Luke

8:19–21	89
11:27–28	88–89
16:18	79–82

1 Corinthians

6:12–20	30, 57
7	82–83
7:1–7	63
7:12–24	85, 108
7:13–16	92
7:39–40	83, 85
11:3–16	67–72
14:33–40	73–74

2 Corinthians

6:14–16	85
11:2	25, 27, 49, 146

Galatians

3:28	67, 99

Scripture Index